on
the Art of Making Up One's Mind

Jerome K. Jerome
on
the Art of Making Up
One's Mind

ET REMOTISSIMA PROPE

'on'

'on'
Published by Hesperus Press Limited
4 Rickett Street, London sw6 1ru
www.hesperuspress.com

First published in *The Second Thoughts of an Idle Fellow*, 1898
This collection first published by Hesperus Press Limited, 2009

Designed and typeset by Fraser Muggeridge studio

ISBN: 978-1-84391-607-9

Contents

Foreword

'By the Author of *Three Men in a Boat*' – how Jerome K. Jerome so utterly loathed this (as he saw it) damnable accolade, plastered as it was across the covers and even the title pages of almost every one of his subsequent books. And even today, many would be surprised to know that he ever did write anything else – understandable really, when one considers that it was published in 1889, has never since been out of print, and no other work by Jerome has ever achieved anything close to its fame and eternal success (this true even in his lifetime, and hence his resentment of the constant reminder). Parallels exist: Arthur Conan Doyle came to regard Sherlock Holmes in much the same way, as did A.A. Milne with Winnie & Co. Baffling to the modern outlook – how can an author mind having created something deathless? In the case of Jerome, the answer is complex. His absolute hero and role-model was Charles Dickens (he suggests in his memoirs, *My Life and Times*, 1926, that as a child he encountered the Great Man in a London park, this leaving him with an indelible impression) and Jerome's long, largely autobiographical novel *Paul Kelver* (1902) was ultimately a homage – his not wholly discreditable attempt at *David Copperfield*. But long before this time Jerome had been irrevocably branded as 'the Author of *Three Men in a Boat*', and he came to regard this sobriquet solely as the robber of any claim to 'seriousness' in his sober and more thoughtful work, of which there was a great deal (and, latterly, rather too much). And while it might be going rather far to suggest that here was the clown who yearned to play Hamlet, it is nonetheless true that Jerome would instantly and gladly have traded in his entire body of work (including *Three Men in a Boat*) together with what reputation he possessed in return for the ultimate prize of having written just one single book that had changed men's thinking. Iris Murdoch might well have understood: at the peak of her success in the 1970s she saw only regret in that she had failed to create a solitary character as memorable as any by Dickens.

But the tagline 'by the Author of *Three Men in a Boat*' Jerome saw as not just a lazy device in order to render his later work what these days would be termed more 'marketable', but as positively detrimental and counterproductive. The preview of his eventually extremely successful and serious play *The Passing of the Third Floor Back* proved a total disaster due to its billing as being 'by the Author of …', the audience having struggled through each of its three acts straining to detect something even remotely comical. In a foreword to an 1894 volume of stories, *John Ingerfield*, Jerome was moved to instruct the reader (and critic) not to judge them from the standpoint of humour, the earnestness almost painfully palpable within his gentle couching of language.

The truth is, of course, that while Jerome was a more than competent writer of drama and even of tragedy, it is in humour – arch, whimsical or riotous – that he excelled. He was not just a fine exponent of the form, but an absolute innovator – the true inventor, really, of what came to be dubbed 'The New Humour', and – because of its appealing slanginess and a directness star-tlingly ahead of its time – earned him the disparaging nickname 'Arry K. 'Arry from the rather snobbish *Punch* magazine. And if *Three Men in a Boat* was undeniably his finest hour, it was by no means his only. This novel was in fact his eighth published work, his inimitable (although much imitated) style having been firmly established three years earlier with a delightful collection of essays, *The Idle Thoughts of an Idle Fellow* – this title pre-empting a memorable few sentences from *Three Men in a Boat*: 'I like work; it fascinates me. I can sit and look at it for hours. I love to keep it by me; the idea of getting rid of it nearly breaks my heart.' Well Jerome did get rid of it, only to replace it with more: a less inert idler never lived. But in common with many determined and hardworking people, Jerome rather enjoyed this image of being The Idler (later founding a periodical bearing that very title), but the plain truth is that he always worked with a ferocity that was very much driven by his fear of ever again being reduced to the penury of his very grim childhood (his background too he identified strongly with that of Dickens). These 'Idle' essays had previously been the star feature in a magazine called *Home Chimes*, and were very much the work of a carefree, talented and innovative humorist in his mid-20s, their audacity – in terms of both attitude and language – very funny, and often breathtaking. Jerome's intention here was solely to divert and amuse, as he makes clear in the preface: 'What readers ask nowadays in a book is that it should improve, instruct and elevate. This book wouldn't elevate a cow.' All this, it must be remembered, was many years before the Grossmiths' *The Diary of a Nobody*, and when P.G. Wodehouse was five years old: the Victorians had never seen anything like it.

The essays that follow this foreword are taken from the lesser-known sequel *The Second Thoughts of an Idle Fellow* – though by sequel we should not infer that here was a rushed-out cashing-in on the rapid success of the initial collection. Twelve years separated the two, during which Jerome had published not just *Three Men in a Boat* but four separate plays, three books of essays and observations, two volumes of short stories and the better-known *The Diary of a Pilgrimage*, a novel based upon an actual journey – the dry run, as it were, for *Three Men in a Boat* (in all, he published forty books and plays). By the time *The Second Thoughts of an Idle Fellow* was published, Jerome was nearly forty and a great deal had happened in his life. He was happily married and very recently had become the father of a daughter. His fame was considerable, and the money he had amassed, in great part due to the already innumerable editions of *Three Men in a Boat*, had enabled him to set up and edit two magazines – *The Idler*, which came out monthly, and a weekly, *To-Day*. This latter magazine was sued for libel – a case too complicated to go into or even comprehend (even Jerome –

never a great businessman – was utterly baffled by it), but the upshot was that although the plaintiff was awarded damages of just one farthing, Jerome had to bear his own costs in what had transpired to be the longest libel case ever heard at the Court of Queen's Bench in the last fifty years. These costs, £9000 (this in 1897) financially ruined him, and both the magazines folded. I mention this because a new sort of colouring now is discernible in each of the Second Thoughts, many more shades and nuances amid the humour – the title, of course, suggesting not just a sequel, but the reconsiderations of a much older man (a vein that runs through the essays like a stubborn and recurrent rheum). Indeed, in 'On the Inadvisability of Following Advice', there is what can only be a very rueful reflection on experience, despite the truth and comedy in it; 'An old gentleman whose profession it was to give legal advice, and excellent legal advice he always gave', has this to say:

'My dear sir, if a villain stopped me in the street and demanded of me my watch and chain, I should refuse to give it to him. If he thereupon said, "Then I shall take it from you by brute force," I should, old as I am, I feel convinced, reply to him, "Come on." But if, on the other hand, he were to say to me, "Very well, then I shall take proceedings against you in the Court of Queen's Bench to compel you to give it up to me," I should at once take it from my pocket, press it into his hand, and beg him to say no more about the matter. And I should consider I was getting off cheaply.'

This essay is actually the funniest of the bunch, featuring as it does an irate gentleman's encounter with an obstinate slot machine and a superb narration concerning a hopelessly inebriated carthorse – very much mainstream Jerome. The other essays here are rather gentler in form and approach and, Jerome would have you believe, written by a man considerably older than forty. This partial adoption of the traditional essayist's attitude – that of a white-bearded sage passing on the wisdom of his accumulated years – contrasts well with the more than occasional purely Jeromian interruption, such as (in 'On the Disadvantage of Not Getting What One Wants') 'One feels the modern Temple of Love must be a sort of Swan & Edgar's'. The theme of this essay is common to most of them – that dreams are better than attainment. Jerome was proud of his achievements, but forever guilty about having and enjoying the fruits of them, constantly insisting that humble is always best – in substance as well as in behaviour. He is strong too on underlining his belief that youth and poverty are often preferable to wealth and experience (perhaps forgetting what poor youths such as he once was might have to say about that). Here is his musing on the subject of 'Fate' from 'On the Exceptional Merit Attaching to the Things We Meant To Do': 'She flung us a few shillings and hope, where now she doles us out pounds and fears.' The worst crime of all, though, he sees to be not complacency but vanity, his fear of succumbing to it always compelling him to (jocularly) belittle his success and the baubles it has brought him, if never his talent. Throughout these essays there is also an assumption that he, the author, is a world-wise man, while still prone to foolishness, addressing a peer. In 'On the Art of Making Up One's Mind' he opens with a wholly amusing dialogue concerning the dithering of women, and then goes on to exhort his audience thus: 'Come, my superior male friend…'. While this is only half ironical, it is not to suggest that he did regard women to be in any way inferior: on the contrary, he was constantly in awe of them. But he knew and was pleased with the fact that they were different, the gulf between the sexes providing a fathomless source of humour, observation and reflection. That said, he would always be happier in a roomful of likeminded gentlemen, much cigar smoke, burgundy and chops, rather than attending a polite recital.

At the time he wrote the essays in this book, Jerome was – despite his financial problems (which proved to be temporary)

– a contented man. But the timbre of his writing was now and perceptibly beginning to alter. He had not, nor would he ever, abandon humour, and neither was he ashamed of being one of its foremost exponents. He found increasingly, however, that there were some thoughts within him to be expressed, some morals to be drawn, that simply could not be accomplished through comedy. These essays form the transitional stage, and are all the more interesting for that. The humour that remains did not become cynical, but it was demonstrably less zesty – and nor did he feel any more that every essay must close in lighter vein, or with the climax of a joke; rather that it should be thought-provoking, and even poignant. The philosophies he expounds here are neither particularly novel nor earth-shaking, but his skill as a writer comes strongly into play in the way in which these many truisms are imparted: he seduces the more than willing reader into having second thoughts. Which, at this stage of his life, was really all he meant.

– *Joseph Connolly, 2009*

On the Art of Making Up One's Mind

On the Art of Making Up One's Mind

'Now, which would you advise, dear? You see, with the red I shan't be able to wear my magenta hat.'

'Well then, why not have the grey?'

'Yes – yes, I think the grey will be more useful.'

'It's a good material.'

'Yes, and it's a pretty grey. You know what I mean, dear; not a *common* grey. Of course grey is always an uninteresting colour.'

'It's quiet.'

'And then again, what I feel about the red is that it is so warm-looking. Red makes you feel warm even when you're not warm. You know what I mean, dear!'

'Well then, why not have the red? It suits you – red.'

'No, do you really think so?'

'Well, when you've got a colour, I mean, of course!'

'Yes, that is the drawback to red. No, I think, on the whole, the grey is safer.'

'Then you will take the grey, madam?'

'Yes, I think I'd better, don't you, dear?'

'I like it myself very much.'

'And it is good wearing stuff. I shall have it trimmed with – oh! you haven't cut it off, have you?'

'I was just about to, madam.'

'Well, don't for a moment. Just let me have another look at the red. You see, dear, it has just occurred to me – that chinchilla would look so well on the red!'

'So it would, dear!'

'And, you see, I've got the chinchilla.'

'Then have the red. Why not?'

'Well, there is the hat I'm thinking of.'

'You haven't anything else you could wear with that?'

'Nothing at all, and it would go so beautifully with the grey. Yes, I think I'll have the grey. It's always a safe colour – grey.'

'Fourteen yards I think you said, madam?'

'Yes, fourteen yards will be enough; because I shall mix it with – one minute. You see, dear, if I take the grey I shall have nothing to wear with my black jacket.'

'Won't it go with grey?'

'Not well – not so well as with red.'

'I should have the red then. You evidently fancy it yourself.'

'No, personally I prefer the grey. But then one must think of everything, and – good gracious! That's surely not the right time?'

'No, madam, it's ten minutes slow. We always keep our clocks a little slow!'

'And we were to have been at Madame Jannaway's at a quarter past twelve. How long shopping does take! Why, whatever time did we start?'

'About eleven, wasn't it?'

'Half past ten. I remember now, because, you know, we said we'd start at half past nine. We've been two hours already!'

'And we don't seem to have done much, do we?'

'Done literally nothing, and I meant to have done so much. I must go to Madame Jannaway's. Have you got my purse, dear? Oh, it's all right, I've got it.'

'Well, now you haven't decided whether you're going to have the grey or the red.'

'I'm sure I don't know what I do want now. I had made up my mind a minute ago, and now it's all gone again – oh yes, I remember, the red. Yes, I'll have the red. No, I don't mean the red, I mean the grey.'

'You were talking about the red last time, if you remember, dear.'

'Oh, so I was, you're quite right. That's the worst of shopping. Do you know I get quite confused sometimes.'

'Then you will decide on the red, madam?'

'Yes – yes, I shan't do any better, shall I, dear? What do you think? You haven't got any other shades of red, have you? This is such an ugly red.'

The shopman reminds her that she has seen all the other reds, and that this is the particular shade she selected and admired.

'Oh, very well,' she replies, with the air of one from whom all earthly cares are falling, 'I must take that then, I suppose. I can't be worried about it any longer. I've wasted half the morning already.'

Outside she recollects three insuperable objections to the red, and four unanswerable arguments why she should have selected the grey. She wonders would they change it, if she went back and asked to see the shopwalker? Her friend, who wants her lunch, thinks not.

'That is what I hate about shopping,' she says. 'One never has time to really think.'

She says she shan't go to that shop again.

We laugh at her, but are we so very much better? Come, my superior male friend, have you never stood, amid your wardrobe, undecided whether, in her eyes, you would appear more imposing, clad in the rough tweed suit that so admirably displays your broad shoulders, or in the orthodox black frock, that, after all, is perhaps more suitable to the figure of a man approaching – let us say, the nine-and-twenties? Or, better still, why not riding costume? Did we not hear her say how well Jones looked in his top-boots and breeches, and, 'hang it all,' we have a better leg than Jones. What a pity riding breeches are made so baggy nowadays. Why is it that male fashions tend more and more to hide the male leg? As women have become less and less ashamed of theirs, we have become more and more reticent of ours. Why are the silken hose, the tight-fitting pantaloons, the neat knee breeches of our forefathers impossible today? Are we grown more modest – or has there come about a falling off, rendering concealment advisable?

I can never understand, myself, why women love us. It must be our honest worth, our sterling merit, that attracts them – certainly not our appearance, in a pair of tweed 'dittos', black angora coat and vest, stand-up collar, and chimney-pot hat! No, it must be our sheer force of character that compels their admiration.

What a good time our ancestors must have had was borne in upon me when, on one occasion, I appeared in character at a fancy dress ball. What I represented I am unable to say, and I don't particularly care. I only know it was something military. I also remember that the costume was two sizes too small for me in the chest and thereabouts, and three sizes too large for me in the hat. I padded the hat, and dined in the middle of the day off a chop and half a glass of soda water. I have gained prizes as a boy for mathematics, also for scripture history – not often, but I have done it. A literary critic, now dead, once praised a book of mine. I know there have been occasions when my conduct has won the approbation of good men, but never – never in my whole life, have I felt more proud, more satisfied with myself than on that evening when, the last hook fastened, I gazed at my full-length self in the cheval glass. I was a dream. I say it who should not, but I am not the only one who said it. I was a glittering dream. The groundwork was red, trimmed with gold braid wherever there was room for gold braid. and where there was no more possible room for gold braid there hung gold cords, and tassels, and straps. Gold buttons and buckles fastened me, gold embroidered belts and sashes caressed me, white horse-hair plumes waved o'er me. I am not sure that everything was in its proper place, but I managed to get everything on somehow, and I looked well. It suited me. My success was a revelation to me of female human nature. Girls who had hitherto been cold and distant gathered round me, timidly solicitous of notice. Girls on whom I smiled lost their heads and gave themselves airs. Girls who were not introduced to me sulked and were rude to girls that had been. For one poor child, with whom I sat out two dances (at least she sat, while I stood gracefully beside her – I had been advised, by the costumier, not to sit), I was sorry. He was a worthy young fellow, the son of a cotton broker, and he would have made her a good husband, I feel sure. But he was foolish to come as a beer bottle.

Perhaps, after all, it is as well those old fashions have gone out. A week in that suit might have impaired my natural modesty.

One wonders that fancy dress balls are not more popular in this grey age of ours. The childish instinct to 'dress up', to 'make believe', is with us all. We grow so tired of being always ourselves. A tea table discussion, at which I once assisted, fell into this: would any one of us, when it came to the point, change with anybody else, the poor man with the millionaire, the governess with the princess – change not only outward circumstances and surroundings, but health and temperament, heart, brain, and soul, so that not one mental or physical particle of one's original self one would retain, save only memory? The general opinion was that we would not, but one lady maintained the affirmative.

'Oh no, you wouldn't really, dear,' argued a friend, 'you *think* you would.'

'Yes, I would,' persisted the first lady, 'I am tired of myself. I'd even be you, for a change.'

In my youth, the question chiefly important to me was: what sort of man shall I decide to be? At nineteen one asks oneself this question. At thirty-nine we say, 'I wish fate hadn't made me this sort of man.'

In those days I was a reader of much well-meant advice to young men, and I gathered that, whether I should become a Sir Lancelot, a Herr Teufelsdröckh, or an Iago was a matter for my own individual choice. Whether I should go through life gaily or gravely was a question the pros and cons of which I carefully considered. For patterns I turned to books. Byron was then still popular, and many of us made up our minds to be gloomy, saturnine young men, weary with the world, and prone to soliloquy. I determined to join them.

For a month I rarely smiled, or, when I did, it was with a weary, bitter smile, concealing a broken heart – at least that was the intention. Shallow-minded observers misunderstood.

'I know exactly how it feels,' they would say, looking at me sympathetically, 'I often have it myself. It's the sudden change in the weather, I think,' and they would press neat brandy upon me, and suggest ginger.

Again, it is distressing to the young man, busy burying his secret sorrow under a mound of silence, to be slapped on the back by commonplace people and asked, 'Well, how's "the hump" this morning?' and to hear his mood of dignified melancholy referred to, by those who should know better, as 'the sulks'.

There are practical difficulties also in the way of him who would play the Byronic young gentleman. He must be super-naturally wicked – or rather must have been, only, alas! in the unliterary grammar of life, where the future tense stands first, and the past is formed, not from the indefinite, but from the present indicative, 'to have been' is 'to be', and to be wicked on a small income is impossible. The ruin of even the simplest of maidens costs money. In the Courts of Love one cannot sue *in forma pauperis*;[1] nor would it be the Byronic method.

'To drown remembrance in the cup' sounds well, but then the 'cup', to be fitting, should be of some expensive brand. To drink deep of old Tokay or Asti is poetical, but when one's purse necessitates that the draught, if it is to be deep enough to drown anything, should be of thin beer at five-and-nine the four and a half gallon cask, or something similar in price, sin is robbed of its flavour.

Possibly also – let me think it – the conviction may have been within me that vice, even at its daintiest, is but an ugly, sordid thing, repulsive in the sunlight; that though – as rags and dirt to art – it may afford picturesque material to literature, it is an evil-smelling garment to the wearer, one that a good man, by reason of poverty of will, may come down to, but one to be avoided with all one's effort, discarded with returning mental prosperity.

Be this as it may, I grew weary of training for a saturnine young man, and, in the midst of my doubt, I chanced upon a book the hero of which was a debonair young buck, own cousin to Tom and Jerry. He attended fights, both of cocks and men, flirted with actresses, wrenched off doorknockers, extinguished street lamps, played many a merry jest upon many an unappreciative night watchman. For all the which he was much beloved by the women of the book. Why should not I flirt with actresses, put out street lamps, play pranks on policemen, and be beloved? London life was changed since the days of my hero, but much remained, and the heart of woman is eternal. If no longer prizefighting was to be had, at least there were boxing competitions, so called, in dingy back parlours out Whitechapel way. Though cockfighting was a lost sport, were there not damp cellars near the river where for twopence a gentleman might back mongrel terriers to kill rats against time, and feel himself indeed a sportsman? True, the atmosphere of reckless gaiety, always surrounding my hero, I missed myself from these scenes, finding in its place an atmosphere more suggestive of gin, stale tobacco, and nervous apprehension of the police, but the essentials must have been the same, and the next morning I could exclaim in the very words of my prototype, 'Odd's crickets, but I feel as though the devil himself were in my head. Peste take me for a fool.'

But in this direction likewise my fatal lack of means opposed me. (It affords much food to the philosophic mind, this influence of income upon character.) Even fifth-rate 'boxing competitions', organised by 'friendly leads', and ratting contests in Rotherhithe slums, become expensive, when you happen to be the only gentleman present possessed of a collar, and are expected to do the honours of your class in dog's nose. True, climbing lampposts and putting out the gas is fairly cheap, providing always you are not caught in the act, but as a recreation it lacks variety. Nor is the modern London lamppost adapted to sport. Anything more difficult to grip – anything with less 'give' in it – I have rarely clasped. The disgraceful amount of dirt allowed to accumulate upon it is another drawback from the climber's point of view. By the time you have swarmed up your third post a positive distaste for 'gaiety' steals over you. Your desire is towards arnica and a bath.

Nor in jokes at the expense of policemen is the fun entirely on your side. Maybe I did not proceed with judgment. It occurs to me now, looking back, that the neighbourhoods of Covent Garden and Great Marlborough Street were ill chosen for sport of this nature. To bonnet a fat policeman is excellent fooling. While he is struggling with his helmet you can ask him comic questions, and by the time he has got his head free you are out of sight. But the game should be played in a district where there is not an average of three constables to every dozen square yards. When two other policemen, who have had their eye on you for the past ten minutes, are watching the proceedings from just round the next corner, you have little or no leisure for due enjoyment of the situation. By the time you have run the whole length of Great Titchfield Street and twice round Oxford Market, you are of opinion that a joke should never be prolonged beyond the point at which there is danger of its becoming wearisome, and that the time has now arrived for home and friends. The 'law', on the other hand, now raised by reinforcements to a strength of six or seven men, is just beginning to enjoy the chase. You picture to yourself, while doing Hanover Square, the scene in Court the next morning. You will be accused of being drunk and disorderly. It will be idle for you to explain to the magistrate (or to your relations afterwards) that you were only trying to live up to a man who did this sort of thing in a book and was admired for it. You will be fined the usual forty shillings, and on the next occasion of your calling at the Mayfields' the girls will be out, and Mrs Mayfield, an excellent lady, who has always taken a motherly interest in you, will talk seriously to you and urge you to sign the pledge.

Thanks to your youth and constitution you shake off the pursuit at Notting Hill, and, to avoid any chance of unpleasant contretemps on the return journey, walk home to Bloomsbury by way of Camden Town and Islington.

I abandoned sportive tendencies as the result of a vow made by myself to Providence, during the early hours of a certain Sunday morning, while clinging to the waterspout of an unpretentious house situate in a side street off Soho. I put it to Providence as man to man. 'Let me only get out of this,' I think were the muttered words I used, 'and no more "sport" for me.' Providence closed on the offer, and did let me get out of it. True, it was a complicated 'get out', involving a broken skylight and three gas globes, two hours in a coal cellar and a sovereign to a potman for the loan of an ulster, and when at last, secure in my chamber, I took stock of myself – what was left of me – I could not but reflect that Providence might have done the job neater. Yet I experienced no desire to escape the terms of the covenant. My inclining for the future was towards a life of simplicity.

Accordingly, I cast about for a new character, and found one to suit me. The German professor was becoming popular as a hero about this period. He wore his hair long and was otherwise untidy, but he had 'a heart of steel', occasionally of gold. The majority of folks in the book, judging him from his exterior together with his conversation – in broken English, dealing chiefly with his dead mother and his little sister Lisa – dubbed him uninteresting, but then they did not know about the heart. His chief possession was a lame dog which he had rescued from a brutal mob; and when he was not talking broken English he was nursing this dog.

But his speciality was stopping runaway horses, thereby saving the heroine's life. This, combined with the broken English and the dog, rendered him irresistible.

He seemed a peaceful, amiable sort of creature, and I decided to try him. I could not of course be a German professor, but I could, and did, wear my hair long in spite of much public advice to the contrary, voiced chiefly by small boys. I endeavoured to obtain possession of a lame dog, but failed. A one-eyed dealer in Seven Dials, to whom, as a last resource, I applied, offered to lame one for me for an extra five shillings, but this suggestion I declined. I came across an uncanny-looking mongrel late one night. He was not lame, but he seemed pretty sick, and, feeling I was not robbing anybody of anything very valuable, I lured him home and nursed him. I fancy I must have over-nursed him. He got so healthy in the end, there was no doing anything with him. He was an ill-conditioned cur, and he was too old to be taught. He became the curse of the neighbourhood. His idea of sport was killing chickens and sneaking rabbits from outside poulterers' shops. For recreation he killed cats and frightened small children by yelping round their legs. There were times when I could have lamed him myself, if only I could have got hold of him. I made nothing by running that dog – nothing whatever. People, instead of admiring me for nursing him back to life, called me a fool, and said that if I didn't drown the brute they would. He spoilt my character utterly – I mean my character at this period. It is difficult to pose as a young man with a heart of gold, when discovered in the middle of the road throwing stones at your own dog. And stones were the only things that would reach and influence him.

I was also hampered by a scarcity in runaway horses. The horse of our suburb was not that type of horse. Once and only once did an opportunity offer itself for practice. It was a good opportunity, inasmuch as he was not running away very greatly. Indeed, I doubt if he knew himself that he was running away. It transpired afterwards that it was a habit of his, after waiting for his driver outside the Rose and Crown for what he considered to be a reasonable period, to trot home on his own account. He passed me going about seven miles an hour, with the reins dragging conveniently beside him. He was the very thing for a beginner, and I prepared myself. At the critical moment, however, a couple of officious policemen pushed me aside and did it themselves.

There was nothing for me to regret, as the matter turned out. I should only have rescued a bald-headed commercial traveller, very drunk, who swore horribly, and pelted the crowd with empty collar-boxes.

From the window of a very high flat I once watched three men, resolved to stop a runaway horse. Each man marched deliberately into the middle of the road and took up his stand. My window was too far away for me to see their faces, but their attitude suggested heroism unto death. The first man, as the horse came charging towards him, faced it with his arms spread out. He never flinched until the horse was within about twenty yards of him. Then, as the animal was evidently determined to continue its wild career, there was nothing left for him to do but to retire again to the kerb, where he stood looking after it with evident sorrow, as though saying to himself, 'Oh, well, if you are going to be headstrong I have done with you.'

The second man, on the catastrophe being thus left clear for him, without a moment's hesitation, walked up a bystreet and disappeared. The third man stood his ground, and, as the horse passed him, yelled at it. I could not hear what he said. I have not the slightest doubt it was excellent advice, but the animal was apparently too excited even to listen. The first and the third man met afterwards, and discussed the matter sympathetically. I judged they were regretting the pig-headed-ness of runaway horses in general, and hoping that nobody had been hurt.

I forget the other characters I assumed about this period. One, I know, that got me into a good deal of trouble was that of a downright, honest, hearty, outspoken young man who always said what he meant.

I never knew but one man who made a real success of speaking his mind. I have heard him slap the table with his open hand and exclaim:

'You want me to flatter you – to stuff you up with a pack of lies. That's not me, that's not Jim Compton. But if you care for my honest opinion, all I can say is, that child is the most marvellous performer on the piano I've ever heard. I don't say she is a genius, but I have heard Liszt and Metzler and all the crack players, and I prefer her. That's my opinion. I speak my mind, and I can't help it if you're offended.'

'How refreshing,' the parents would say, 'to come across a man who is not afraid to say what he really thinks. Why are we not all outspoken?'

The last character I attempted I thought would be easy to assume. It was that of a much admired and beloved young man, whose great charm lay in the fact that he was always just – himself. Other people posed and acted. He never made any effort to be anything but his own natural, simple self.

I thought I also would be my own natural, simple self. But then the question arose: what was my own natural, simple self?

That was the preliminary problem I had to solve. I have not solved it to this day. What am I? I am a great gentleman, walking through the world with dauntless heart and head erect, scornful of all meanness, impatient of all littleness. I am a mean-thinking, little-daring man – the type of man that I of the dauntless heart and the erect head despise greatly – crawling to a poor end by devious ways, cringing to the strong, timid of all pain. I – but, dear reader, I will not sadden your sensitive ears with details I could give you, showing how contemptible a creature this wretched I happens to be. Nor would you understand me. You would only be astonished, discovering that such disreputable specimens of humanity contrive to exist in this age. It is best, my dear sir, or madam, you should remain ignorant of these evil persons. Let me not trouble you with knowledge.

I am a philosopher, greeting alike the thunder and the sunshine with frolic welcome. Only now and then, when all things do not fall exactly as I wish them, when foolish, wicked people will persist in doing foolish, wicked acts, affecting my comfort and happiness, I rage and fret a goodish deal.

As Heine said of himself, I am knight, too, of the Holy Grail, valiant for the Truth, reverent of all women, honouring all men, eager to yield life to the service of my great Captain.

And next moment, I find myself in the enemy's lines, fighting under the black banner. (It must be confusing to these opposing Generals, all their soldiers being deserters from both armies.) What are women but men's playthings! Shall there be no more cakes and ale for me because thou art virtuous! What are men but hungry dogs, contending each against each for a limited supply of bones! Do others lest thou be done. What is the truth but an unexploded lie!

I am a lover of all living things. You, my poor sister, struggling with your heavy burden on your lonely way, I would kiss the tears from your worn cheeks, lighten with my love the darkness around your feet. You, my patient brother, breathing hard as round and round you tramp the trodden path, like some poor half-blind gin-horse, stripes your only encouragement, scanty store of dry chaff in your manger! I would jog beside you, taking the strain a little from your aching shoulders; and we would walk nodding, our heads side by side, and you, remembering, should tell me of the fields where long ago you played, of the gallant races that you ran and won. And you, little pinched brats, with wondering eyes, looking from dirt-encrusted faces, I would take you in my arms and tell you fairy stories. Into the sweet land of make-believe we would wander, leaving the sad old world behind us for a time, and you should be princes and princesses, and know love.

But again, a selfish, greedy man comes often, and sits in my clothes. A man who frets away his life, planning how to get more money – more food, more clothes, more pleasures for himself, a man so busy thinking of the many things he needs he has no time to dwell upon the needs of others. He deems himself the centre of the universe. You would imagine, hearing him grumbling, that the world had been created and got ready against the time when he should come to take his pleasure in it.

He would push and trample, heedless, reaching towards these many desires of his, and when, grabbing, he misses, he curses Heaven for its injustice, and men and women for getting in his path. He is not a nice man, in any way. I wish, as I say, he would not come so often and sit in my clothes. He persists that he is I, and that I am only a sentimental fool, spoiling his chances. Sometimes, for a while, I get rid of him, but he always comes back, and then he gets rid of me and I become him. It is very confusing. Sometimes I wonder if I really am myself.

On the Disadvantage of Not Getting What One Wants

Long, long ago, when you and I, dear Reader, were young, when the fairies dwelt in the hearts of the roses, when the moonbeams bent each night beneath the weight of angels' feet, there lived a good, wise man. Or rather, I should say, there had lived, for at the time of which I speak the poor old gentleman lay dying. Waiting each moment the dread summons, he fell a-musing on the life that stretched far back behind him. How full it seemed to him at that moment of follies and mistakes, bringing bitter tears not to himself alone but to others also. How much brighter a road might it have been, had he been wiser, had he known!

'Ah, me!' said the good old gentleman, 'if only I could live my life again in the light of experience.'

Now as he spoke these words he felt the drawing near to him of a Presence, and thinking it was the One whom he expected, raising himself a little from his bed, he feebly cried, 'I am ready.'

But a hand forced him gently back, a voice saying, 'Not yet. I bring life, not death. Your wish shall be granted. You shall live your life again, and the knowledge of the past shall be with you to guide you. See you use it. I will come again.'

Then a sleep fell upon the good man, and when he awoke, he was again a little child, lying in his mother's arms, but locked within his brain was the knowledge of the life that he had lived already.

So once more he lived and loved and laboured. So a second time he lay an old, worn man with life behind him. And the angel stood again beside his bed, and the voice said, 'Well, are you content now?'

'I am well content,' said the old gentleman. 'Let Death come.'

'And have you understood?' asked the angel.

'I think so,' was the answer, 'that experience is but as of the memory of the pathways he has trod to a traveller journeying ever onward into an unknown land. I have been wise only to reap the reward of folly. Knowledge has oft-times kept me from my good. I have avoided my old mistakes only to fall into others that I knew not of. I have reached the old errors by new roads. Where I have escaped sorrow I have lost joy. Where I have grasped happiness I have plucked pain also. Now let me go with Death that I may learn.'

Which was so like the angel of that period, the giving of a gift, bringing to a man only more trouble. Maybe I am overrating my coolness of judgment under somewhat startling circumstances, but I am inclined to think that, had I lived in those days, and had a fairy or an angel come to me, wanting to give me something – my soul's desire, or the sum of my ambition, or any trifle of that kind – I should have been short with him.

'You pack up that precious bag of tricks of yours,' I should have said to him (it would have been rude, but that is how I should have felt), 'and get outside with it. I'm not taking anything in your line today. I don't require any supernatural aid to get me into trouble. All the worry I want I can get down here, so it's no good your calling. You take that little joke of yours – I don't know what it is, but I know enough not to want to know – and run it off on some other idiot. I'm not priggish. I have no objection to an innocent game of "catch-questions" in the ordinary way, and when I get a turn myself. But if I've got to pay every time, and the stakes are to be my earthly happiness plus my future existence – why, I don't play. There was the case of Midas – a nice, shabby trick you fellows played off upon him! Making pretence you did not understand him, twisting round the poor old fellow's words, just for all the world as though you were a pack of Old Bailey lawyers, trying to trip up a witness. I'm ashamed of the lot of you, and I tell you so – coming down here, fooling poor unsuspecting mortals with your nonsense, as though we had not enough to harry us as it was. Then there was that other case of the poor old peasant couple to whom you promised three wishes, the whole thing ending in a black pudding. And they never got even that. You thought that funny, I suppose. That was your fairy humour! A pity, I say, you have not, all of you, something better to do with your time. As I said before, you take that celestial "Joe Miller" of yours and work it off on somebody else. I have read my fairy lore, and I have read my mythology, and I don't want any of your blessings. And what's more, I'm not going to have them. When I want blessings I will put up with the usual sort we are accustomed to down here. You know the ones I mean, the disguised brand – the blessings that no human being would think were blessings, if he were not told, the blessings that don't look like blessings, that don't feel like blessings, that, as a matter of fact, are not blessings, practically speaking. The blessings that other people think are blessings for us and that we don't. They've got their drawbacks, but they are better than yours, at any rate, and they are sooner over. I don't want your blessings at any price. If you leave one here I shall simply throw it out after you.'

I feel confident I should have answered in that strain, and I feel it would have done good. Somebody ought to have spoken plainly, because with fairies and angels of that sort fooling about, no one was ever safe for a moment. Children could hardly have been allowed outside the door. One never could have told what silly trick some would-be funny fairy might be waiting to play off on them. The poor child would not know, and would think it was getting something worth having. The wonder to me is that some of those angels didn't get tarred and feathered.

I am doubtful whether even Cinderella's luck was quite as satisfying as we are led to believe. After the carpetless kitchen and the black beetles, how beautiful the palace must have seemed – for the first year, perhaps for the first two. And the Prince! how loving, how gallant, how tender – for the first year, perhaps for the first two. And after? You see he was a prince, brought up in a court, the atmosphere of which is not conducive to the development of the domestic virtues, and she – was Cinderella. And then the marriage altogether was rather a hurried affair. Oh yes, she is a good, loving little woman, but perhaps our Royal Highness-ship did act too much on the impulse of the moment. It was her dear, dainty feet that danced their way into our heart. How they flashed and twinkled, cased in those fairy slippers. How like a lily among tulips she moved that night amid the over-gorgeous court dames. She was so sweet, so fresh, so different to all the others whom we knew so well. How happy she looked as she put her trembling little hand in ours. What possibilities might lie behind those drooping lashes. And we were in amorous mood that night, the music in our feet, the flash and glitter in our eyes. And then, to pique us further, she disappeared as suddenly and strangely as she had come. Who was she? Whence came she? What was the mystery surrounding her? Was she only a delicious dream, a haunting fantasy that we should never look upon again, never clasp again within our longing arms? Was our heart to be for ever hungry, haunted by the memory of – no, by heavens, she is real, and a woman. Here is her dear slipper, made surely to be kissed. Of a size too that a man may well wear within the breast of his doublet. Had any woman – nay, fairy, angel, such dear feet! Search the whole kingdom through, but find her, find her. The gods have heard our prayers, and given us this clue. 'Suppose she be not all she seemed. Suppose she be not of birth fit to mate with our noble house!' Out upon thee, for an earthbound, blind curmudgeon of a Lord High Chancellor. How could a woman, whom such slipper fitted, be but of the noblest and the best, as far above us, mere princelet that we are, as the stars in heaven are brighter than thy dull old eyes! Go, search the kingdom, we tell thee, from east to west, from north to south, and see to it that thou findest her, or it shall go hard with thee. By Venus, be she a swineherd's daughter, she shall be our queen – if she deign to accept of us, and of our kingdom.

Ah well, of course, it was not a wise piece of business, that goes without saying; but we were young, and princes are only human. Poor child, she could not help her education, or rather

her lack of it. Dear little thing, the wonder is that she has contrived to be no more ignorant than she is, dragged up as she was, neglected and overworked. Nor does life in a kitchen, amid the companionship of peasants and menials, tend to foster the intellect. Who can blame her for being shy and somewhat dull of thought? Not we, generous-minded, kind-hearted prince that we are. And she is very affectionate. The family are trying, certainly: father-in-law not a bad sort, though a little prosy when upon the subject of his domestic troubles, and a little too fond of his glass; mamma-in-law, and those two ugly, ill-mannered sisters, decidedly a nuisance about the palace. Yet what can we do? They are our relations now, and they do not forget to let us know it. Well, well, we had to expect that, and things might have been worse. Anyhow she is not jealous, thank goodness.

So the day comes when poor little Cinderella sits alone of a night in the beautiful palace. The courtiers have gone home in their carriages. The Lord High Chancellor has bowed himself out backwards. The Gold-Stick-in-Waiting and the Grooms of the Chamber have gone to their beds. The Maids of Honour have said 'Goodnight,' and drifted out of the door, laughing and whispering among themselves. The clock strikes twelve – one – two, and still no footstep creaks upon the stair. Once it followed swiftly upon the 'goodnight' of the maids, who did not laugh or whisper then.

At last the door opens, and the Prince enters, none too pleased at finding Cinderella still awake. 'So sorry I'm late, my love – detained on affairs of state. Foreign policy very complicated, dear. Have only just this moment left the Council Chamber.'

And little Cinderella, while the Prince sleeps, lies sobbing out her poor sad heart into the beautiful royal pillow, embroidered with the royal arms and edged with the royal monogram in lace. 'Why did he ever marry me? I should have been happier in the old kitchen. The black beetles did frighten me a little, but there was always the dear old cat, and sometimes, when mother and the girls were out, papa would call softly down the kitchen stairs for me to come up, and we would have such a merry evening together, and sup off sausages. Dear old dad, I hardly ever see him now. And then, when my work was done, how pleasant it was to sit in front of the fire, and dream of the wonderful things that would come to me some day. I was always going to be a Princess, even in my dreams, and live in a palace, but it was so different to this. Oh, how I hate it, this beastly palace where everybody sneers at me, I know they do, though they bow and scrape, and pretend to be so polite. And I'm not clever and smart as they are. I hate them. I hate these bold-faced women who are always here. That is the worst of a palace, everybody can come in. Oh, I hate everybody and everything. Oh, god-mamma, god-mamma, come and take me away. Take me back to my old kitchen. Give me back my old poor frock. Let me dance again with the fire-tongs for a partner, and be happy, dreaming.'

Poor little Cinderella, perhaps it would have been better had god-mamma been less ambitious for you, dear; had you married some good, honest yeoman, who would never have known that you were not brilliant, who would have loved you because you were just amiable and pretty; had your kingdom been only a farmhouse, where your knowledge of domestic economy, gained so hardly, would have been useful, where you would have shone instead of being overshadowed, where Papa would have dropped in of an evening to smoke his pipe and escape from his domestic wrangles, where you would have been real queen.

But then you know, dear, you would not have been content. Ah yes, with your present experience, now you know that queens as well as little drudges have their troubles, but without that experience? You would have looked in the glass when you were alone, you would have looked at your shapely hands and feet, and the shadows would have crossed your pretty face. 'Yes,' you would have said to yourself, 'John is a dear, kind fellow, and I love him very much, and all that, but – ' and the old dreams, dreamt in the old low-ceilinged kitchen before the dying fire, would have come back to you, and you would have been discontented then as now, only in a different way. Oh yes, you would, Cinderella, though you gravely shake your gold-crowned head. And let me tell you why. It is because you are a woman, and the fate of all us, men and women alike, is to be for ever wanting what we have not, and to be finding, when we have it, that it is not what we wanted. That is the law of life, dear. Do you think as you lie upon the floor with your head upon your arms, that you are the only woman whose tears are soaking into the hearthrug at that moment? My dear Princess, if you could creep unseen about your city, peeping at will through the curtain-shielded windows, you would come to think that all the world was little else than a big nursery full of crying children with none to comfort them. The doll is broken: no longer it sweetly squeaks in answer to our pressure, 'I love you, kiss me.' The drum lies silent with the drumstick inside. No longer do we make a brave noise in the nursery. The box of tea things we have clumsily put our foot upon; there will be no more merry parties around the three-legged stool. The tin trumpet will not play the note we want to sound, the wooden bricks keep falling down, the toy cannon has exploded and burnt our fingers. Never mind, little man, little woman, we will try and mend things tomorrow.

And after all, Cinderella dear, you do live in a fine palace, and you have jewels and grand dresses and – no, no, do not be indignant with me. Did not you dream of these things as well as of love? Come now, be honest. It was always a prince, was it not, or, at the least, an exceedingly well-to-do party, that handsome young gentleman who bowed to you so gallantly from the red embers? He was never a virtuous young commercial traveller, or cultured clerk, earning a salary of three pounds a week, was he, Cinderella? Yet there are many charming commercial travellers, many delightful clerks with limited incomes, quite sufficient, however, to a sensible man and woman desiring but each other's love. Why was it always a prince, Cinderella?

Had the palace and the liveried servants, and the carriages and horses, and the jewels and the dresses, nothing to do with the dream?

No, Cinderella, you were human, that is all. The artist, shivering in his conventional attic, dreaming of fame, do you think he is not hoping she will come to his loving arms in the form Jove came to Danae? Do you think he is not reckoning also upon the good dinners and the big cigars, the fur coat and the diamond studs, that her visits will enable him to purchase?

There is a certain picture very popular just now. You may see it, Cinderella, in many of the shop windows of the town. It is called 'The Dream of Love', and it represents a beautiful young girl, sleeping in a very beautiful but somewhat disarranged bed. Indeed, one hopes, for the sleeper's sake, that the night is warm, and that the room is fairly free from draughts. A ladder of light streams down from the sky into the room, and upon this ladder crowd and jostle one another a small army of plump Cupids, each one laden with some pledge of love. Two of the imps are emptying a sack of jewels upon the floor. Four others are bearing, well displayed, a magnificent dress (a 'confection', I believe, is the proper term) cut somewhat low, but making up in train what is lacking elsewhere. Others bear bonnet boxes from which peep stylish toques and bewitching hoods. Some, representing evidently wholesale houses, stagger under silks and satins in the piece. Cupids are there from the shoemakers with the daintiest of bottines. Stockings, garters, and even less mentionable articles, are not forgotten. Caskets, mirrors, twelve-buttoned gloves, scent bottles and handkerchiefs, hairpins, and the gayest of parasols, has the God of Love piled into the arms of his messengers. Really a most practical, up-to- date God of Love, moving with the times! One feels that the modern Temple of Love must be a sort of Swan and Edgar's, the god himself a kind of celestial shop walker, while his mother, Venus, no doubt superintends the costume department. Quite an Olympian Whiteley, this latter-day Eros. He has forgotten nothing, for, at the back of the picture, I notice one Cupid carrying a rather fat heart at the end of a string.

You, Cinderella, could give good counsel to that sleeping child. You would say to her: 'Awake from such dreams. The contents of a pawnbroker's storeroom will not bring you happiness. Dream of love if you will; that is a wise dream, even if it remain ever a dream. But these coloured beads, these Manchester goods! Are you then – you, heiress of all the ages – still at heart only as some poor savage maiden but little removed above the monkeys that share the primeval forest with her? Will you sell your gold to the first trader that brings you *this* barter? These things, child, will only dazzle your eyes for a few days. Do you think the Burlington Arcade is the gate of Heaven?'

Ah, yes, I too could talk like that, I, writer of books, to the young lad, sick of his office stool, dreaming of a literary career leading to fame and fortune. 'And do you think, lad, that by that road you will reach happiness sooner than by another? Do you think interviews with yourself in penny weeklies will bring you any satisfaction after the first half-dozen? Do you think the gushing female who has read all your books, and who wonders what it must feel like to be so clever, will be welcome to you the tenth time you meet her? Do you think press cuttings will always consist of wondering admiration of your genius, of paragraphs about your charming personal appearance under the heading, "Our Celebrities"? Have you thought of the *un*-complimentary criticisms, of the spiteful paragraphs, of the everlasting fear of slipping a few inches down the greasy pole called "popular taste", to which you are condemned to cling for life, as some lesser criminal to his weary treadmill, struggling with no hope but not to fall! Make a home, lad, for the woman who loves you; gather one or two friends about you; work, think, and play, that will bring you happiness. Shun this roaring gingerbread fair that calls itself, forsooth, the "World of art and letters". Let its clowns and its contortionists fight among themselves for the plaudits and the halfpence of the mob. Let it be with its shouting and its surging, its blare and its cheap flare. Come away, the summer's night is just the other side of the hedge, with its silence and its stars.'

You and I, Cinderella, are experienced people, and can therefore offer good advice, but do you think we should be listened to?

'Ah, no, my Prince is not as yours. Mine will love me always, and I am peculiarly fitted for the life of a palace. I have the instinct and the ability for it. I am sure I was made for a princess. Thank you, Cinderella, for your well-meant counsel, but there is much difference between you and me.'

That is the answer you would receive, Cinderella, and my young friend would say to me, 'Yes, I can understand *your* finding disappointment in the literary career, but then, you see, our cases are not quite similar. I am not likely to find much trouble in keeping my position. I shall not fear reading what the critics say of me. No doubt there are disadvantages, when you are among the ruck, but there is always plenty of room at the top. So thank you, and goodbye.'

Besides, Cinderella dear, we should not quite mean it, this excellent advice. We have grown accustomed to these gew-gaws, and we should miss them in spite of our knowledge of their trashiness – you, your palace and your little gold crown; I, my mountebank's cap, and the answering laugh that goes up from the crowd when I shake my bells. We want everything. All the happiness that earth and heaven are capable of bestowing. Creature comforts, and heart and soul comforts also, and, proud-spirited beings that we are, we will not be put off with a part. Give us only everything, and we will be content. And, after all, Cinderella, you have had your day. Some little dogs never get theirs. You must not be greedy. You have known happiness. The palace was paradise for those few months, and the Prince's arms were about you, Cinderella, the Prince's kisses on your lips. The gods themselves cannot take that from you.

The cake cannot last for ever if we will eat of it so greedily. There must come the day when we have picked hungrily the last crumb – when we sit staring at the empty board, nothing left of the feast, Cinderella, but the pain that comes of feasting.

It is a naive confession poor human nature has made to itself, in choosing, as it has, this story of Cinderella for its leading moral: be good, little girl. Be meek under your many trials. Be gentle and kind, in spite of your hard lot, and one day, you shall marry a prince and ride in your own carriage. Be brave and true, little boy. Work hard and wait with patience, and in the end, with God's blessing, you shall earn riches enough to come back to London town and marry your master's daughter.

You and I, gentle Reader, could teach these young folks a truer lesson, if we would. We know, alas, that the road of all the virtues does not lead to wealth, rather the contrary, else how explain our limited incomes? But would it be well, think you, to tell them bluntly the truth, that honesty is the most expensive luxury a man can indulge in? That virtue, if persisted in, leads, generally speaking, to a six-roomed house in an outlying sub-urb? Maybe the world is wise: the fiction has its uses.

I am acquainted with a fairly intelligent young lady. She can read and write, knows her tables up to six times, and can argue. I regard her as representative of average humanity in its attitude towards fate, and this is a dialogue I lately overheard between her and an older lady who is good enough to occasionally impart to her the wisdom of the world:

'I've been good this morning, haven't I?'

'Yes, oh yes, fairly good, for you.'

'You think Papa will take me to the circus tonight?'

'Yes, if you keep good. If you don't get naughty this afternoon.'

A pause.

'I was good on Monday, you may remember, nurse.'

'Tolerably good.'

'Very good, you said, nurse.'

'Well, yes, you weren't bad.'

'And I was to have gone to the pantomime, and I didn't.'

'Well, that was because your aunt came up suddenly, and your Papa couldn't get another seat. Poor auntie wouldn't have gone at all if she hadn't gone then.'

'Oh, wouldn't she?'

'No.'

Another pause.

'Do you think she'll come up suddenly today?'

'Oh no, I don't think so.'

'No, I hope she doesn't. I want to go to the circus tonight. Because, you see, nurse, if I don't it will discourage me.'

So, perhaps the world is wise in promising us the circus. We believe her at first. But after a while, I fear, we grow discouraged.

On the Exceptional Merit Attaching to the Things We Meant to Do

I can remember – but then I can remember a long time ago. You, gentle Reader, just entering upon the prime of life, that age by thoughtless youth called middle, I cannot, of course, expect to follow me – when there was in great demand a certain periodical ycleped *The Amateur*. Its aim was noble. It sought to teach the beautiful lesson of independence, to inculcate the fine doctrine of self-help. One chapter explained to a man how he might make flowerpots out of Australian meat cans, another how he might turn butter tubs into music stools, a third how he might utilise old bonnet boxes for Venetian blinds: that was the principle of the whole scheme, you made everything from something not intended for it, and as ill suited to the purpose as possible.

Two pages, I distinctly recollect, were devoted to the encouragement of the manufacture of umbrella stands out of old gas-piping. Anything less adapted to the receipt of hats and umbrellas than gas-piping I cannot myself conceive: had there been, I feel sure the author would have thought of it, and would have recommended it.

Picture frames you fashioned out of ginger beer corks. You saved your ginger beer corks, you found a picture – and the thing was complete. How much ginger beer it would be necessary to drink, preparatory to the making of each frame; and the effect of it upon the frame-maker's physical, mental and moral well-being, did not concern *The Amateur*. I calculate that for a fair-sized picture sixteen dozen bottles might suffice. Whether, after sixteen dozen of ginger beer, a man would take any interest in framing a picture – whether he would retain any pride in the picture itself, is doubtful. But this, of course, was not the point.

One young gentleman of my acquaintance – the son of the gardener of my sister, as friend Ollendorff would have described him – did succeed in getting through sufficient ginger beer to frame his grandfather, but the result was not encouraging. Indeed, the gardener's wife herself was but ill satisfied.

'What's all them corks round father?' was her first question.

'Can't you see?' Was the somewhat indignant reply, 'that's the frame.'

'Oh! but why corks?'

'Well, the book said corks.'

Still the old lady remained unimpressed.

'Somehow it don't look like father now,' she sighed.

Her eldest born grew irritable: none of us appreciate criticism!

'What does it look like, then?' he growled.

'Well, I dunno. Seems to me to look like nothing but corks.'

The old lady's view was correct. Certain schools of art possibly lend themselves to this method of framing. I myself have seen a funeral card improved by it, but, generally speaking, the consequence was a predominance of frame at the expense of the thing framed. The more honest and tasteful of the frame-makers would admit as much themselves.

'Yes, it is ugly when you look at it,' said one to me, as we stood surveying it from the centre of the room. 'But what one feels about it is that one has done it oneself.'

Which reflection, I have noticed, reconciles us to many other things beside cork frames.

Another young gentleman friend of mine – for I am bound to admit it was youth that profited most by the advice and counsel of *The Amateur*: I suppose as one grows older one grows less daring, less industrious – made a rocking chair, according to the instructions of this book, out of a couple of beer barrels. From every practical point of view it was a bad rocking chair. It rocked too much, and it rocked in too many directions at one and the same time. I take it, a man sitting on a rocking chair does not want to be continually rocking. There comes a time when he says to himself, 'Now I have rocked sufficiently for the present, now I will sit still for a while, lest a worse thing befall me.' But this was one of those headstrong rocking chairs that are a danger to humanity, and a nuisance to themselves. Its notion was that it was made to rock, and that when it was not rocking, it was wasting its time. Once started nothing could stop it – nothing ever did stop it, until it found itself topsy-turvy on its own occupant. That was the only thing that ever sobered it.

I had called, and had been shown into the empty drawing room. The rocking chair nodded invitingly at me. I never guessed it was an amateur rocking chair. I was young in those days, with faith in human nature, and I imagined that, whatever else a man might attempt without knowledge or experience, no one would be fool enough to experiment upon a rocking chair.

I threw myself into it lightly and carelessly. I immediately noticed the ceiling. I made an instinctive movement forward. The window and a momentary glimpse of the wooded hills beyond shot upwards and disappeared. The carpet flashed across my eyes, and I caught sight of my own boots vanishing beneath me at the rate of about two hundred miles an hour. I made a convulsive effort to recover them. I suppose I overdid it. I saw the whole of the room at once, the four walls, the ceiling, and the floor at the same moment. It was a sort of vision. I saw the cottage piano upside down, and I again saw my own boots flash past me, this time over my head, soles uppermost. Never before had I been in a position where my own boots had seemed so all-pervading. The next moment I lost my boots, and stopped the carpet with my head just as it was rushing past me. At the same instant something hit me violently in the small of the back. Reason, when recovered, suggested that my assailant must be the rocking chair.

Investigation proved the surmise correct. Fortunately I was still alone, and in consequence was able, a few minutes later, to meet my hostess with calm and dignity. I said nothing about the rocking chair. As a matter of fact, I was hoping to have the pleasure, before I went, of seeing some other guest arrive and sample it: I had purposely replaced it in the most prominent and convenient position. But though I felt capable of schooling myself to silence, I found myself unable to agree with my hostess when she called for my admiration of the thing. My recent experiences had too deeply embittered me.

'Willie made it himself,' explained the fond mother. 'Don't you think it was very clever of him?'

'Oh yes, it was clever,' I replied, 'I am willing to admit that.'

'He made it out of some old beer barrels,' she continued. She seemed proud of it.

My resentment, though I tried to keep it under control, was mounting higher.

'Oh! Did he?' I said, 'I should have thought he might have found something better to do with them.'

'What?' she asked.

'Oh! Well, many things,' I retorted. 'He might have filled them again with beer.'

My hostess looked at me astonished. I felt some reason for my tone was expected.

'You see,' I explained, 'it is not a well-made chair. These rockers are too short, and they are too curved, and one of them, if you notice, is higher than the other and of a smaller radius. The back is at too obtuse an angle. When it is occupied the centre of gravity becomes –'

My hostess interrupted me.

'You have been sitting on it,' she said.

'Not for long,' I assured her.

Her tone changed. She became apologetic.

'I am so sorry,' she said. 'It looks all right.'

'It does,' I agreed, 'that is where the dear lad's cleverness displays itself. Its appearance disarms suspicion. With judgment that chair might be made to serve a really useful purpose. There are mutual acquaintances of ours – I mention no names, you will know them – pompous, self-satisfied, superior persons who would be improved by that chair. If I were Willie I should disguise the mechanism with some artistic drapery, bait the thing with a couple of exceptionally inviting cushions, and employ it to inculcate modesty and diffidence. I defy any human being to get out of that chair, feeling as important as when he got into it. What the dear boy has done has been to construct an automatic exponent of the transitory nature of human greatness. As a moral agency that chair should prove a blessing in disguise.'

My hostess smiled feebly, more, I fear, from politeness than genuine enjoyment.

'I think you are too severe,' she said. 'When you remember that the boy has never tried his hand at anything of the kind before, that he has no knowledge and no experience, it really is not so bad.'

Considering the matter from that point of view I was bound to concur. I did not like to suggest to her that before entering upon a difficult task it would be better for young men to *acquire* knowledge and experience: that is so unpopular a theory.

But the thing that *The Amateur* put in the front and foremost of its propaganda was the manufacture of household furniture out of egg-boxes. Why egg-boxes I have never been able to understand, but egg-boxes, according to the prescription of *The Amateur*, formed the foundation of household existence. With a sufficient supply of egg-boxes, and what *The Amateur* termed a 'natural deftness', no young couple need hesitate to face the furnishing problem. Three egg-boxes made a writing-table, on another egg-box you sat to write, your books were ranged in egg-boxes around you – and there was your study, complete.

For the dining room two egg-boxes made an overmantel, four egg-boxes and a piece of looking glass a sideboard, while six egg-boxes, with some wadding and a yard or so of cretonne, constituted a so-called 'cosy corner'. About the 'corner' there could be no possible doubt. You sat on a corner, you leant against a corner; whichever way you moved you struck a fresh corner. The 'cosiness', however, I deny. Egg-boxes I admit can be made useful, I am even prepared to imagine them ornamental, but 'cosy', no. I have sampled egg-boxes in many shapes. I speak of years ago, when the world and we were younger, when our fortune was the future, secure in which we hesitated not to set up house upon incomes folks with lesser expectations might have deemed insufficient. Under such circumstances, the sole alternative to the egg-box, or similar school of furniture, would have been the strictly classical, consisting of a doorway joined to architectural proportions.

I have from Saturday to Monday, as honoured guest, hung my clothes in egg-boxes.

I have sat on an egg-box at an egg-box to take my dish of tea. I have made love on egg-boxes. Aye, and to feel again the blood running through my veins as then it ran, I would be content to sit only on egg-boxes till the time should come when I could be buried in an egg-box, with an egg-box reared above me as tombstone. I have spent many an evening on an egg-box; I have gone to bed in egg-boxes. They have their points – I am intending no pun – but to claim for them cosiness would be but to deceive.

How quaint they were, those homemade rooms! They rise out of the shadows and shape themselves again before my eyes. I see the knobbly sofa, the easy chairs that might have been designed by the Grand Inquisitor himself, the dented settle that was a bed by night, the few blue plates purchased in the slums off Wardour Street, the enamelled stool to which one always stuck, the mirror framed in silk, the two Japanese fans crossed beneath each cheap engraving, the piano cloth embroidered in peacock's feathers by Annie's sister, the teacloth worked by Cousin Jenny. We dreamt, sitting on those egg-boxes – for we were young ladies and gentlemen with artistic taste – of the days when we would eat in Chippendale dining rooms, sip our coffee in Louis Quatorze drawing rooms, and be happy. Well, we have got on, some of us, since then, as Mr Bumpus used to say; and

I notice, when on visits, that some of us have contrived so that we do sit on Chippendale chairs, at Sheraton dining tables, and are warmed from Adam's fireplaces, but, ah me, where are the dreams, the hopes, the enthusiasms that clung like the scent of a March morning about those gimcrack second floors? In the dustbin, I fear, with the cretonne-covered egg-boxes and the penny fans. Fate is so terribly even handed. As she gives she ever takes away. She flung us a few shillings and hope, where now she doles us out pounds and fears. Why did not we know how happy we were, sitting crowned with sweet conceit upon our egg-box thrones?

Yes, Dick, you have climbed well. You edit a great newspaper. You spread abroad the message – well, the message that Sir Joseph Goldbug, your proprietor, instructs you to spread abroad. You teach mankind the lessons that Sir Joseph Goldbug wishes them to learn. They say he is to have a peerage next year. I am sure he has earned it, and perhaps there may be a knighthood for you, Dick.

Tom, you are getting on now. You have abandoned those unsaleable allegories. What rich art patron cares to be told continually by his own walls that Midas had ass' ears, that Lazarus sits ever at the gate? You paint portraits now, and everybody tells me you are the coming man. That 'Impression' of old Lady Jezebel was really wonderful. The woman looks quite handsome, and yet it is her ladyship. Your touch is truly marvellous.

But into your success, Tom – Dick, old friend, do not there creep moments when you would that we could fish up those old egg-boxes from the past, refurnish with them the dingy rooms in Camden Town, and find there our youth, our loves, and our beliefs?

An incident brought back to my mind, the other day, the thought of all these things. I called for the first time upon a man, an actor, who had asked me to come and see him in the little home where he lives with his old father. To my astonishment – for the craze, I believe, has long since died out – I found the house half furnished out of packing cases, butter tubs, and egg-boxes. My friend earns his twenty pounds a week, but it was the old father's hobby, so he explained to me, the making of these monstrosities, and of them he was as proud as though they were specimen furniture out of the South Kensington Museum.

He took me into the dining room to show me the latest outrage – a new bookcase. A greater disfigurement to the room, which was otherwise prettily furnished, could hardly be imagined. There was no need for him to assure me, as he did, that it had been made out of nothing but egg-boxes. One could see at a glance that it was made out of egg-boxes, and badly constructed egg-boxes at that – egg-boxes that were a disgrace to the firm that had turned them out, egg-boxes not worthy the storage of 'shop 'uns' at eighteen the shilling.

We went upstairs to my friend's bedroom. He opened the door as a man might open the door of a museum of gems.

'The old boy,' he said, as he stood with his hand upon the doorknob, 'made everything you see here, everything,' and we entered. He drew my attention to the wardrobe. 'Now I will hold it up,' he said, 'while you pull the door open, I think the floor must be a bit uneven, it wobbles if you are not careful.' It wobbled notwithstanding, but by coaxing and humouring we succeeded without mishap. I was surprised to notice a very small supply of clothes within, although my friend is a dressy man.

'You see,' he explained, 'I dare not use it more than I can help. I am a clumsy chap, and as likely as not, if I happened to be in a hurry, I'd have the whole thing over,' which seemed probable.

I asked him how he contrived. 'I dress in the bathroom as a rule,' he replied, 'I keep most of my things there. Of course the old boy doesn't know.'

He showed me a chest of drawers. One drawer stood half open.

'I'm bound to leave that drawer open,' he said, 'I keep the things I use in that. They don't shut quite easily, these drawers – or rather, they shut all right, but then they won't open. It is the weather, I think. They will open and shut all right in the summer, I dare say.' He is of a hopeful disposition.

But the pride of the room was the washstand.

'What do you think of this?' cried he enthusiastically, 'real marble top – '

He did not expatiate further. In his excitement he had laid his hand upon the thing, with the natural result that it collapsed. More by accident than design I caught the jug in my arms. I also caught the water it contained. The basin rolled on its edge and little damage was done, except to me and the soapbox.

I could not pump up much admiration for this washstand. I was feeling too wet.

'What do you do when you want to wash?' I asked, as together we reset the trap.

There fell upon him the manner of a conspirator revealing secrets. He glanced guiltily round the room, then, creeping on tiptoe, he opened a cupboard behind the bed. Within was a tin basin and a small can.

'Don't tell the old boy,' he said. 'I keep these things here, and wash on the floor.'

That was the best thing I myself ever got out of egg-boxes – that picture of a deceitful son stealthily washing himself upon the floor behind the bed, trembling at every footstep lest it might be the 'old boy' coming to the door.

One wonders whether the Ten Commandments are so all-sufficient as we good folk deem them – whether the eleventh is not worth the whole pack of them: 'that ye love one another' with just a commonplace, human, practical love. Could not the other ten be comfortably stowed away into a corner of that! One is inclined, in one's anarchic moments, to agree with Louis Stevenson, that to be amiable and cheerful is a good religion for a workaday world. We are so busy *not* killing, *not* stealing, *not* coveting our neighbour's wife, we have not time to be even just to one another for the little while we are together here. Need we be so cocksure that our present list of virtues and vices is the only possibly correct and complete one? Is the kind, unselfish man necessarily a villain because he does not always succeed in suppressing his natural instincts? Is the narrow-hearted, sour-souled man, incapable of a generous thought or act, necessarily a saint because he has none? Have we not – we *unco guid*[2] – arrived at a wrong method of estimating our frailer brothers and sisters? We judge them, as critics judge books, not by the good that is in them, but by their faults. Poor King David! What would the local Vigilance Society have had to say to him? Noah, according to our plan, would be denounced from every teetotal platform in the country, and Ham would head the Local Vestry poll as a reward for having exposed him. And St Peter! Weak, frail St Peter, how lucky for him that his fellow disciples and their Master were not as strict in their notions of virtue as are we today.

Have we not forgotten the meaning of the word 'virtue'? Once it stood for the good that was in a man, irrespective of the evil that might lie there also, as tares among the wheat. We have abolished virtue, and for it substituted virtues. Not the hero – he was too full of faults – but the blameless valet, not the man who does any good, but the man who has not been found out in any evil, is our modern ideal. The most virtuous thing in nature, according to this new theory, should be the oyster. He is always at home, and always sober. He is not noisy. He gives no trouble to the police. I cannot think of a single one of the Ten Commandments that he ever breaks. He never enjoys himself, and he never, so long as he lives, gives a moment's pleasure to any other living thing.

I can imagine the oyster lecturing a lion on the subject of morality.

'You never hear me,' the oyster might say, 'howling round camps and villages, making night hideous, frightening quiet folk out of their lives. Why don't you go to bed early, as I do? I never prowl round the oyster-bed, fighting other gentlemen oysters, making love to lady oysters already married. I never kill antelopes or missionaries. Why can't you live as I do on salt water and germs, or whatever it is that I do live on? Why don't you try to be more like me?'

An oyster has no evil passions, therefore we say he is a virtuous fish. We never ask ourselves, 'Has he any good passions?' A lion's behaviour is often such as no just man could condone. Has he not his good points also?

Will the fat, sleek, 'virtuous' man be as welcome at the gate of heaven as he supposes?

'Well,' St Peter may say to him, opening the door a little way and looking him up and down, 'what is it now?'

'It's me,' the virtuous man will reply, with an oily, self-satisfied smile, 'I should say, I – I've come.'

'Yes, I see you have come; but what is your claim to admittance? What have you done with your three score years and ten?'

'Done!' the virtuous man will answer, 'I have done nothing, I assure you.'

'Nothing!'

'Nothing. That is my strong point, that is why I am here. I have never done any wrong.'

'And what good have you done?'

'What good!'

'Aye, what good? Do not you even know the meaning of the word? What human creature is the better for your having eaten and drunk and slept these years? You have done no harm – no harm to yourself. Perhaps if you had you might have done some good with it. The two are generally to be found together down below, I remember. What good have you done that you should enter here? This is no mummy chamber, this is the place of men and women who have lived, who have wrought good – and evil also, alas! – for the sinners who fight for the right, not the righteous who run with their souls from the fight.'

It was not, however, to speak of these things that I remembered *The Amateur* and its lessons. My intention was but to lead up to the story of a certain small boy, who in the doing of tasks not required of him was exceedingly clever. I wish to tell you his story, because, as do most true tales, it possesses a moral, and stories without a moral I deem to be but foolish literature, resembling roads that lead to nowhere, such as sick folk tramp for exercise.

I have known this little boy to take an expensive eight-day clock to pieces, and make of it a toy steamboat. True, it was not, when made, very much of a steamboat, but taking into consideration all the difficulties – the inadaptability of eight-day clock machinery to steamboat requirements, the necessity of getting the work accomplished quickly, before conservatively minded people with no enthusiasm for science could interfere – a good enough steamboat. With merely an ironing board and a few dozen meat-skewers, he would – provided the ironing board was not missed in time – turn out quite a practicable rabbit hutch. He could make a gun out of an umbrella and a gas bracket, which, if not so accurate as a Martini-Henry, was, at all events, more deadly. With half the garden hose, a copper scalding-pan out of the dairy, and a few Dresden china ornaments off the drawing room mantelpiece, he would build a fountain for the garden. He could make bookshelves out of kitchen tables, and crossbows out of crinolines. He could dam you a stream so that all the water would flow over the croquet lawn. He knew how to make red paint and oxygen gas, together with many other suchlike commodities handy to have about a house. Among other things he learned how to make fireworks, and after a few explosions of an unimportant character, came to make them very well indeed. The boy who can play a good game of cricket is liked. The boy who can fight well is respected. The boy who can cheek a master is loved. But the boy who can make fireworks is revered above all others as a boy belonging to a superior order of beings. The fifth of November was at hand, and with the consent of an indulgent mother, he determined to give to the world a proof of his powers. A large party of friends, relatives, and schoolmates was invited, and for a fortnight beforehand the scullery was converted into a manufactory for fireworks. The female servants went about in hourly terror of their lives, and the villa, did we judge exclusively by smell, one might have imagined had been taken over by Satan, his main premises being inconveniently crowded, as an annex. By the evening of the fourth all was in readiness, and samples were tested to make sure that no contretemps should occur the following night. All was found to be perfect. The rockets rushed heavenward and descended in stars, the Roman candles tossed their fiery balls into the darkness, the Catherine wheels sparkled and whirled, the crackers cracked, and the squibs banged. That night he went to bed a proud and happy boy, and dreamed of fame. He stood surrounded by blazing fireworks, and the vast crowd cheered him. His relations, most of whom, he knew, regarded him as the coming idiot of the family, were there to witness his triumph, so too was Dickey Bowles, who laughed at him because he could not throw straight. The girl at the bun shop, she also was there, and saw that he was clever.

The night of the festival arrived, and with it the guests. They sat, wrapped up in shawls and cloaks, outside the hall door – uncles, cousins, aunts, little boys and big boys, little girls and big girls, with, as the theatre posters say, villagers and retainers, some forty of them in all, and waited.

But the fireworks did not go off. Why they did not go off I cannot explain, nobody ever could explain. The laws of nature seemed to be suspended for that night only. The rockets fell down and died where they stood. No human agency seemed able to ignite the squibs. The crackers gave one bang and collapsed. The Roman candles might have been English rushlights. The Catherine wheels became mere revolving glow-worms. The fiery serpents could not collect among them the spirit of a tortoise. The set piece, a ship at sea, showed one mast and the captain, and then went out. One or two items did their duty, but this only served to render the foolishness of the whole more striking. The little girls giggled, the little boys chaffed, the aunts and cousins said it was beautiful, the uncles inquired if it was all over, and talked about supper and trains, the 'villagers and retainers' dispersed laughing, the indulgent mother said 'never mind', and explained how well everything had gone off yesterday, the clever little boy crept upstairs to his room, and blubbered his heart out in the dark.

Hours later, when the crowd had forgotten him, he stole out again into the garden. He sat down amid the ruins of his hope, and wondered what could have caused the fiasco. Still puzzled, he drew from his pocket a box of matches, and, lighting one, he held it to the seared end of a rocket he had tried in vain to light four hours ago. It smouldered for an instant, then shot with a swish into the air and broke into a hundred points of fire. He tried another and another with the same result. He made a fresh attempt to fire the set piece. Point by point the whole picture – minus the captain and one mast – came out of the night, and stood revealed in all the majesty of flame. Its sparks fell upon the piled-up heap of candles, wheels, and rockets that a little while before had obstinately refused to burn, and that, one after another, had been thrown aside as useless. Now with the night frost upon them, they leaped to light in one grand volcanic eruption. And in front of the gorgeous spectacle he stood with only one consolation – his mother's hand in his.

The whole thing was a mystery to him at the time, but, as he learned to know life better, he came to understand that it was only one example of a solid but inexplicable fact, ruling all human affairs – *your fireworks won't go off while the crowd is around.*

Our brilliant repartees do not occur to us till the door is closed upon us and we are alone in the street, or, as the French would say, are coming down the stairs. Our after-dinner oratory, that sounded so telling as we delivered it before the looking glass, falls strangely flat amidst the clinking of the glasses. The passionate torrent of words we meant to pour into her ear becomes a halting rigmarole, at which – small blame to her – she only laughs.

I would, gentle Reader, you could hear the stories that I meant to tell you. You judge me, of course, by the stories of mine that you have read – by this sort of thing, perhaps, but that is not just to me. The stories I have not told you, that I am going to tell you one day, I would that you judge me by those.

They are so beautiful, you will say so. Over them, you will laugh and cry with me.

They come into my brain unbidden, they clamour to be written, yet when I take my pen in hand they are gone. It is as though they were shy of publicity, as though they would say to me, 'You alone, you shall read us, but you must not write us, we are too real, too true. We are like the thoughts you cannot speak. Perhaps a little later, when you know more of life, then you shall tell us.'

Next to these in merit I would place, were I writing a critical essay on myself, the stories I have begun to write and that remain unfinished, why I cannot explain to myself. They are good stories, most of them, better far than the stories I have accomplished. Another time, perhaps, if you care to listen, I will tell you the beginning of one or two and you shall judge. Strangely enough, for I have always regarded myself as a practical, common-sensed man, so many of these still-born children of my mind I find, on looking through the cupboard where their thin bodies lie, are ghost stories. I suppose the hope of ghosts is with us all. The world grows somewhat interesting to us heirs of all the ages. Year by year, Science with broom and duster tears down the moth-worn tapestry, forces the doors of the locked chambers, lets light into the secret stairways, cleans out the dungeons, explores the hidden passages – finding everywhere only dust. This echoing old castle, the world, so full of mystery in the days when we were children, is losing somewhat its charm for us as we grow older. The king sleeps no longer in the hollow of the hills. We have tunnelled through his mountain chamber.

We have shivered his beard with our pick. We have driven the gods from Olympus. No wanderer through the moonlit groves now fears or hopes the sweet, death-giving gleam of Aphrodite's face. Thor's hammer echoes not among the peaks – 'tis but the thunder of the excursion train. We have swept the woods of the fairies. We have filtered the sea of its nymphs. Even the ghosts are leaving us, chased by the Psychical Research Society.

Perhaps of all, they are the least, however, to be regretted. They were dull old fellows, clanking their rusty chains and groaning and sighing. Let them go.

And yet how interesting they might be, if only they would. The old gentleman in the coat of mail, who lived in King John's reign, who was murdered, so they say, on the outskirts of the very wood I can see from my window as I write – stabbed in the back, poor gentleman, as he was riding home, his body flung into the moat that to this day is called Tor's tomb. Dry enough it is now, and the primroses love its steep banks, but a gloomy enough place in those days, no doubt, with its twenty feet of stagnant water. Why does he haunt the forest paths at night, as they tell me he does, frightening the children out of their wits, blanching the faces and stilling the laughter of the peasant lads and lasses, slouching home from the village dance? Instead, why does he not come up here and talk to me? He should have my easy-chair and welcome, would he only be cheerful and companionable. What brave tales could he not tell me. He fought in the first Crusade, heard the clarion voice of Peter, met the great Godfrey face to face, stood, hand on sword-hilt, at Runnymede, perhaps. Better than a whole library of historical novels would an evening's chat be with such a ghost. What has he done with his eight hundred years of death? Where has he been? What has he seen? Maybe he has visited Mars, has spoken to the strange spirits who can live in the liquid fires of Jupiter. What has he learned of the great secret? Has he found the truth? Or is he, even as I, a wanderer still seeking the unknown?

You, poor, pale, grey nun – they tell me that of midnights one may see your white face peering from the ruined belfry window, hear the clash of sword and shield among the cedar trees beneath.

It was very sad, I quite understand, my dear lady. Your lovers both were killed, and you retired to a convent. Believe me, I am sincerely sorry for you, but why waste every night renewing the whole painful experience? Would it not be better forgotten? Good Heavens, madam, suppose we living folk were to spend our lives wailing and wringing our hands because of the wrongs done to us when we were children? It is all over now. Had he lived, and had you married him, you might not have been happy. I do not wish to say anything unkind, but marriages founded upon the sincerest mutual love have sometimes turned out unfortunately, as you must surely know.

Do take my advice. Talk the matter over with the young men themselves. Persuade them to shake hands and be friends. Come in, all of you, out of the cold, and let us have some reasonable talk.

Why seek you to trouble us, you poor pale ghosts? Are we not your children? Be our wise friends. Tell me, how loved the young men in your young days? how answered the maidens? Has the world changed much, do you think? Had you not new women even then? Girls who hated the everlasting tapestry frame and spinning-wheel? Your father's servants, were they so much worse off than the freemen who live in our East End slums and sew slippers for fourteen hours a day at a wage of nine shillings a week? Do you think Society much improved during the last thousand years? Is it worse? Is it better? Or is it, on the whole, about the same, save that we call things by other names? Tell me, what have *you* learned?

Yet might not familiarity breed contempt, even for ghosts.

One has had a tiring day's shooting. One is looking forward to one's bed. As one opens the door, however, a ghostly laugh comes from behind the bed curtains, and one groans inwardly, knowing what is in store for one: a two or three hours' talk with rowdy old Sir Lanval – he of the lance. We know all his tales by heart, and he will shout them. Suppose our aunt, from whom we have expectations, and who sleeps in the next room, should wake and overhear! They were fit and proper enough stories, no doubt, for the Round Table, but we feel sure our aunt would not appreciate them: that story about Sir Agravain and the cooper's wife! And he always will tell that story.

Or imagine the maid entering after dinner to say:

'Oh, if you please, sir, here is the veiled lady.'

'What, again!' says your wife, looking up from her work.

'Yes, ma'am. Shall I show her up into the bedroom?'

'You had better ask your master,' is the reply. The tone is suggestive of an unpleasant five minutes so soon as the girl shall have withdrawn, but what are you to do?

'Yes, yes, show her up,' you say, and the girl goes out, closing the door.

Your wife gathers her work together, and rises.

'Where are you going?' you ask.

'To sleep with the children,' is the frigid answer.

'It will look so rude,' you urge. 'We must be civil to the poor thing, and you see it really is her room, as one might say. She has always haunted it.'

'It is very curious,' returns the wife of your bosom, still more icily, 'that she never haunts it except when you are down here. Where she goes when you are in town I'm sure I don't know.'

This is unjust. You cannot restrain your indignation.

'What nonsense you talk, Elizabeth,' you reply, 'I am only barely polite to her.'

'Some men have such curious notions of politeness,' returns Elizabeth. 'But pray do not let us quarrel. I am only anxious not to disturb you. Two are company, you know. I don't choose to be the third, that's all.' With which she goes out.

And the veiled lady is still waiting for you upstairs. You wonder how long she will stop, also what will happen after she is gone.

I fear there is no room for you, ghosts, in this our world. You remember how they came to Hiawatha – the ghosts of the departed loved ones. He had prayed to them that they would come back to him to comfort him, so one day they crept into his wigwam, sat in silence round his fireside, chilled the air for Hiawatha, froze the smiles of Laughing Water.

There is no room for you, oh you poor pale ghosts, in this our world. Do not trouble us. Let us forget. You, stout elderly matron, your thin locks turning grey, your eyes grown weak, your chin more ample, your voice harsh with much scolding and complaining, needful, alas! to household management, I pray you leave me. I loved you while you lived. How sweet, how beautiful you were. I see you now in your white frock among the apple-blossom. But you are dead, and your ghost disturbs my dreams. I would it haunted me not.

You, dull old fellow, looking out at me from the glass at which I shave, why do you haunt me? You are the ghost of a bright lad I once knew well. He might have done much, had he lived. I always had faith in him. Why do you haunt me? I would rather think of him as I remember him. I never imagined he would make such a poor ghost.

On the Time Wasted in Looking Before One Leaps

Have you ever noticed the going out of a woman?

When a man goes out, he says, 'I'm going out, shan't be long.'

'Oh, George,' cries his wife from the other end of the house, 'don't go for a moment. I want you to – ' She hears a falling of hats, followed by the slamming of the front door.

'Oh, George, you're not gone!' she wails. It is but the voice of despair. As a matter of fact, she knows he is gone. She reaches the hall, breathless.

'He might have waited a minute,' she mutters to herself, as she picks up the hats, 'there were so many things I wanted him to do.'

She does not open the door and attempt to stop him, she knows he is already halfway down the street. It is a mean, paltry way of going out, she thinks: so like a man.

When a woman, on the other hand, goes out, people know about it. She does not sneak out. She says she is going out. She says it, generally, on the afternoon of the day before; and she repeats it, at intervals, until teatime. At tea, she suddenly decides that she won't, that she will leave it till the day after tomorrow instead. An hour later she thinks she will go tomorrow, after all, and makes arrangements to wash her hair overnight. For the next hour or so she alternates between fits of exaltation, during which she looks forward to going out, and moments of despondency, when a sense of foreboding falls upon her. At dinner she persuades some other woman to go with her; the other woman, once persuaded, is enthusiastic about going, until she recollects that she cannot. The first woman, however, convinces her that she can.

'Yes,' replies the second woman, 'but then, how about you, dear? You are forgetting the Joneses.'

'So I was,' answers the first woman, completely nonplussed.

'How very awkward, and I can't go on Wednesday. I shall have to leave it till Thursday, now.'

'But I can't go Thursday,' says the second woman.

'Well, you go without me, dear,' says the first woman, in the tone of one who is sacrificing a life's ambition.

'Oh no, dear, I should not think of it,' nobly exclaims the second woman. 'We will wait and go together, Friday.'

'I'll tell you what we'll do,' says the first woman. 'We will start early,' (this is an inspiration), 'and be back before the Joneses arrive.'

They agree to sleep together; there is a lurking suspicion in both their minds that this may be their last sleep on earth. They retire early with a can of hot water. At intervals, during the night, one overhears them splashing water, and talking.

They come down very late for breakfast, and both very cross. Each seems to have argued herself into the belief that she has been lured into this piece of nonsense, against her better judgment, by the persistent folly of the other one. During the meal each one asks the other, every five minutes, if she is quite ready. Each one, it appears, has only her hat to put on. They talk about the weather, and wonder what it is going to do. They wish it would make up its mind, one way or the other. They are very bitter on weather that cannot make up its mind. After breakfast it still looks cloudy, and they decide to abandon the scheme altogether. The first woman then remembers that it is absolutely necessary for her, at all events, to go.

'But there is no need for you to come, dear,' she says.

Up to that point the second woman was evidently not sure whether she wished to go or whether she didn't. Now she knows.

'Oh yes, I'll come,' she says, 'then it will be over!'

'I am sure you don't want to go,' urges the first woman, 'and I shall be quicker by myself. I am ready to start now.'

The second woman bridles.

'I shan't be a couple of minutes,' she retorts. 'You know, dear, it's generally I who have to wait for you.'

'But you've not got your boots on,' the first woman reminds her.

'Well, they won't take any time,' is the answer. 'But of course, dear, if you'd really rather I did not come, say so.' By this time she is on the verge of tears.

'Of course, I would like you to come, dear,' explains the first in a resigned tone. 'I thought perhaps you were only coming to please me.'

'Oh no, I'd like to come,' says the second woman.

'Well, we must hurry up,' says the first, 'I shan't be more than a minute myself, I've merely got to change my skirt.'

Half an hour later you hear them calling to each other, from different parts of the house, to know if the other one is ready. It appears they have both been ready for quite a long while, waiting only for the other one.

'I'm afraid,' calls out the one whose turn it is to be downstairs, 'it's going to rain.'

'Oh, don't say that,' calls back the other one.

'Well, it looks very like it.'

'What a nuisance,' answers the upstairs woman, 'shall we put it off?'

'Well, what do you think, dear?' replies the downstairs.

They decide they will go, only now they will have to change their boots, and put on different hats.

For the next ten minutes they are still shouting and running about. Then it seems as if they really were ready, nothing remaining but for them to say 'Goodbye,' and go.

They begin by kissing the children. A woman never leaves her house without secret misgivings that she will never return to it alive. One child cannot be found. When it is found it wishes it hadn't been. It has to be washed, preparatory to being kissed. After that, the dog has to be found and kissed, and final instructions given to the cook.

Then they open the front door.

'Oh, George,' calls out the first woman, turning round again.

'Are you there?'

'Hullo,' answers a voice from the distance. 'Do you want me?'

'No, dear, only to say goodbye. I'm going.'

'Oh, goodbye.'

'Goodbye, dear. Do you think it's going to rain?'

'Oh no, I should not say so.'

'George.'

'Yes.'

'Have you got any money?'

Five minutes later they come running back: the one has forgotten her parasol, the other her purse.

And speaking of purses, reminds one of another essential difference between the male and female human animal. A man carries his money in his pocket. When he wants to use it, he takes it out and lays it down. This is a crude way of doing things, a woman displays more subtlety. Say she is standing in the street, and wants fourpence to pay for a bunch of violets she has purchased from a flower-girl. She has two parcels in one hand, and a parasol in the other. With the remaining two fingers of the left hand she secures the violets. The question then arises, how to pay the girl? She flutters for a few minutes, evidently not quite understanding why it is she cannot do it. The reason then occurs to her: she has only two hands and both these are occupied. First she thinks she will put the parcels and the flowers into her right hand, then she thinks she will put the parasol into her left. Then she looks round for a table or even a chair, but there is not such a thing in the whole street. Her difficulty is solved by her dropping the parcels and the flowers. The girl picks them up for her and holds them. This enables her to feel for her pocket with her right hand, while waving her open parasol about with her left. She knocks an old gentleman's hat off into the gutter, and nearly blinds the flower-girl before it occurs to her to close it. This done, she leans it up against the flower-girl's basket, and sets to work in earnest with both hands. She seizes herself firmly by the back, and turns the upper part of her body round till her hair is in front and her eyes behind. Still holding herself firmly with her left hand – did she let herself go, goodness knows where she would spin to – with her right she prospects herself. The purse is there, she can feel it, the problem is how to get at it. The quickest way would, of course, be to take off the skirt, sit down on the curb, turn it inside out, and work from the bottom of the pocket upwards. But this simple idea never seems to occur to her. There are some thirty folds at the back of the dress, between two of these folds commences the secret passage. At last, purely by chance, she suddenly discovers it, nearly upsetting herself in the process, and the purse is brought up to the surface. The difficulty of opening it still remains. She knows it opens with a spring, but the secret of that spring she has never mastered, and she never will. Her plan is to worry it generally until it does open. Five minutes will always do it, provided she is not flustered.

At last it does open. It would be incorrect to say that she opens it. It opens because it is sick of being mauled about; and, as likely as not, it opens at the moment when she is holding it upside down. If you happen to be near enough to look over her shoulder, you will notice that the gold and silver lies loose within it. In an inner sanctuary, carefully secured with a second secret spring, she keeps her coppers, together with a postage stamp and a draper's receipt, nine months old, for eleven pence, three farthings.

I remember the indignation of an old bus conductor, once. Inside we were nine women and two men. I sat next the door, and his remarks therefore he addressed to me. It was certainly taking him some time to collect the fares, but I think he would have got on better had he been less bustling; he worried them, and made them nervous.

'Look at that,' he said, drawing my attention to a poor lady opposite, who was diving in the customary manner for her purse, 'they sit on their money, women do. Blest if you wouldn't think they was trying to 'atch it.'

At length the lady drew from underneath herself an exceedingly fat purse.

'Fancy riding in a bumpy bus, perched up on that thing,' he continued. 'Think what a stamina they must have.' He grew confidential. 'I've seen one woman,' he said, 'pull out from underneath 'er a street doorkey, a tin box of lozengers, a pencil case, a whopping big purse, a packet of hairpins, and a smelling bottle. Why, you or me would be wretched, sitting on a plain doorknob, and them women goes about like that all day. I suppose they gets used to it. Drop 'em on an eiderdown pillow, and they'd scream. The time it takes me to get tuppence out of them, why, it's 'eartbreaking. First they tries one side, then they tries the other. Then they gets up and shakes theirselves till the bus jerks them back again, and there they are, a more 'opeless 'eap than ever. If I 'ad my way I'd make every bus carry a female searcher as could over'aul 'em one at a time, and take the money from 'em. Talk about the poor pickpocket. What I say is, that a man as finds his way into a woman's pocket – well, he deserves what he gets.'

But it was the thought of more serious matters that lured me into reflections concerning the over-carefulness of women. It is a theory of mine – wrong possibly, indeed I have so been informed – that we pick our way through life with too much care. We are for ever looking down upon the ground. Maybe, we do avoid a stumble or two over a stone or a brier, but also we miss the blue of the sky, the glory of the hills. These books that good men write, telling us that what they call 'success' in life depends on our flinging aside our youth and wasting our manhood in order that we may have the means when we are eighty of spending a rollicking old age, annoy me. We save all our lives to invest in a South Sea Bubble, and in skimping and scheming, we have grown mean, and narrow, and hard. We will put off the gathering of the roses till tomorrow, today it shall be all work, all bargain driving, all plotting. Lo, when tomorrow comes, the roses are blown, nor do we care for roses, idle things of small marketable value. Cabbages are more to our fancy by the time tomorrow comes.

Life is a thing to be lived, not spent; to be faced, not ordered. Life is not a game of chess, the victory to the most knowing; it is a game of cards, one's hand by skill to be made the best of. Is it the wisest who is always the most successful? I think not. The luckiest whist-player I ever came across was a man who was never quite certain what were trumps, and whose most frequent observation during the game was 'I really beg your pardon,' addressed to his partner, a remark which generally elicited the reply:

'Oh, don't apologise. All's well that ends well.'

The man I knew who made the most rapid fortune was a builder in the outskirts of Birmingham, who could not write his name, and who, for thirty years of his life, never went to bed sober. I do not say that forgetfulness of trumps should be cultivated by whist-players. I think my builder friend might have been even more successful had he learned to write his name, and had he occasionally – not overdoing it – enjoyed a sober evening. All I wish to impress is, that virtue is not the road to success – of the kind we are dealing with. We must find other reasons for being virtuous, maybe there are some. The truth is, life is a gamble pure and simple, and the rules we lay down for success are akin to the infallible systems with which a certain class of idiot goes armed each season to Monte Carlo. We can play the game with coolness and judgment, decide when to plunge and when to stake small, but to think that wisdom will decide it, is to imagine that we have discovered the law of chance. Let us play the game of life as sportsmen, pocketing our winnings with a smile, leaving our losings with a shrug. Perhaps that is why we have been summoned to the board and the cards dealt round: that we may learn some of the virtues of the good gambler; his self-control, his courage under misfortune, his modesty under the strain of success, his firmness, his alertness, his general indifference to fate. Good lessons these, all of them. If by the game we learn some of them our time on the green earth has not been wasted. If we rise from the table having learned only fretfulness and self-pity I fear it has been.

The grim Hall Porter taps at the door: 'Number five hundred billion and twenty-eight, your boatman is waiting, sir.'

So! Is it time already? We pick up our counters. Of what use are they? In the country the other side of the river they are no tender. The blood-red for gold, and the pale green for love, to whom shall we fling them? Here is some poor beggar longing to play, let us give them to him as we pass out. Poor devil! The game will amuse him, for a while.

Keep your powder dry, and trust in Providence, is the motto of the wise. Wet powder could never be of any possible use to you. Dry, it may be, with the help of Providence. We will call it Providence; it is a prettier name than Chance, perhaps also a truer.

Another mistake we make when we reason out our lives is this: we reason as though we were planning for reasonable creatures. It is a big mistake. Well-meaning ladies and gentlemen make it when they picture their ideal worlds. When marriage is reformed, and the social problem solved, when poverty and war have been abolished by acclamation, and sin and sorrow rescinded by an overwhelming parliamentary majority! Ah, then the world will be worthy of our living in it. You need not wait, ladies and gentlemen, so long as you think for that time. No social revolution is needed, no slow education of the people is necessary. It would all come about tomorrow, if only we were reasonable creatures.

Imagine a world of reasonable beings! The Ten Commandments would be unnecessary: no reasoning being sins, no reasoning creature makes mistakes. There would be no rich men, for what reasonable man cares for luxury and ostentation? There would be no poor: that I should eat enough for two while my brother in the next street, as good a man as I, starves, is not reasonable. There would be no difference of opinion on any two points: there is only one reason. You, dear Reader, would find, that on all subjects you were of the same opinion as I. No novels would be written, no plays performed: the lives of reasonable creatures do not afford drama. No mad loves, no mad laughter, no scalding tears, no fierce unreasoning, brief-lived joys, no sorrows, no wild dreams, only reason, reason everywhere.

But for the present we remain unreasonable. If I eat this mayonnaise, drink this champagne, I shall suffer in my liver. Then, why do I eat it? Julia is a charming girl, amiable, wise, and witty, also she has a share in a brewery. Then, why does John marry Ann? Who is short tempered, to say the least of it, who, he feels, will not make him so good a housewife, who has extravagant notions, who has no little fortune. There is something about Ann's chin that fascinates him – he could not explain to you what. On the whole, Julia is the better looking of the two. But the more he thinks of Julia, the more he is drawn towards Ann. So Tom marries Julia and the brewery fails, and Julia, on a holiday, contracts rheumatic fever, and is a helpless invalid for life; while Ann comes in for ten thousand pounds left to her by an Australian uncle no one had ever heard of.

I have been told of a young man, who chose his wife with excellent care. Said he to himself, very wisely, 'In the selection of a wife a man cannot be too circumspect.' He convinced himself that the girl was everything a helpmate should be. She had every virtue that could be expected in a woman, no faults, but such as are inseparable from a woman. Speaking practically, she was perfection. He married her, and found she was all he had thought her. Only one thing could he urge against her, that he did not like her. And that, of course, was not her fault.

How easy life would be did we know ourselves. Could we always be sure that tomorrow we should think as we do today. We fall in love during a summer holiday: she is fresh, delightful, altogether charming, the blood rushes to our head every time we think of her. Our ideal career is one of perpetual service at her feet. It seems impossible that fate could bestow upon us any greater happiness than the privilege of cleaning her boots, and kissing the hem of her garment – if the hem be a little muddy that will please us the more. We tell her our ambition, and at that moment every word we utter is sincere. But the summer holiday passes, and with it the holiday mood, and winter finds us wondering how we are going to get out of the difficulty into which we have landed ourselves. Or worse still, perhaps, the mood lasts longer than is usual. We become formally engaged. We marry – I wonder how many marriages are the result of a passion that is burnt out before the altar-rails are reached – and three months afterwards the little lass is broken hearted to find that we consider the lacing of her boots a bore. Her feet seem to have grown bigger. There is no excuse for us, save that we are silly children, never sure of what we are crying for, hurting one another in our play, crying very loudly when hurt ourselves.

I knew an American lady once who used to bore me with long accounts of the brutalities exercised upon her by her husband. She had instituted divorce proceedings against him. The trial came on, and she was highly successful. We all congratulated her, and then for some months she dropped out of my life. But there came a day when we again found ourselves together. One of the problems of social life is to know what to say to one another when we meet; every man and woman's desire is to appear sympathetic and clever, and this makes conversation difficult, because, taking us all round, we are neither sympathetic nor clever – but this by the way.

Of course, I began to talk to her about her former husband. I asked her how he was getting on. She replied that she thought he was very comfortable.

'Married again?' I suggested.

'Yes,' she answered.

'Serve him right,' I exclaimed, 'and his wife too.' She was a pretty, bright-eyed little woman, my American friend, and I wished to ingratiate myself. 'A woman who would marry such a man, knowing what she must have known of him, is sure to make him wretched, and we may trust him to be a curse to her.'

My friend seemed inclined to defend him.

'I think he is greatly improved,' she argued.

'Nonsense!' I returned, 'a man never improves. Once a villain, always a villain.'

'Oh, hush!' she pleaded, 'you mustn't call him that.'

'Why not?' I answered. 'I have heard you call him a villain yourself.'

'It was wrong of me,' she said, flushing. 'I'm afraid he was not the only one to be blamed. We were both foolish in those days, but I think we have both learned a lesson.'

I remained silent, waiting for the necessary explanation.

'You had better come and see him for yourself,' she added, with a little laugh, 'to tell the truth, I am the woman who has married him. Tuesday is my day, Number 2, K— Mansions,' and she ran off, leaving me staring after her.

I believe an enterprising clergyman who would set up a little church in the Strand, just outside the Law Courts, might do quite a trade, remarrying couples who had just been divorced. A friend of mine, a respondent, told me he had never loved his wife more than on two occasions, the first when she refused him, the second when she came into the witness box to give evidence against him.

'You are curious creatures, you men,' remarked a lady once to another man in my presence. 'You never seem to know your own mind.'

She was feeling annoyed with men generally. I do not blame her. I feel annoyed with them myself sometimes. There is one man in particular I am always feeling intensely irritated against. He says one thing, and acts another. He will talk like a saint and behave like a fool, knows what is right and does what is wrong. But we will not speak further of him. He will be all he should be one day, and then we will pack him into a nice, comfortably lined box, and screw the lid down tight upon him, and put him away in a quiet little spot near a church I know of, lest he should get up and misbehave himself again.

The other man, who is a wise man as men go, looked at his fair critic with a smile.

'My dear madam,' he replied, 'you are blaming the wrong person. I confess I do not know my mind, and what little I do know of it I do not like. I did not make it, I did not select it. I am more dissatisfied with it than you can possibly be. It is a greater mystery to me than it is to you, and I have to live with it. You should pity not blame me.'

There are moods in which I fall to envying those old hermits who frankly, and with courageous cowardice, shirked the problem of life. There are days when I dream of an existence unfettered by the thousand petty strings with which our souls lie bound to Lilliputia land. I picture myself living in some Norwegian sater, high above the black waters of a rockbound fjord. No other human creature disputes with me my kingdom. I am alone with the whispering fir forests and the stars. How I live I am not quite sure. Once a month I could journey down into the villages and return laden. I should not need much. For the rest, my gun and fishing rod would supply me. I would have with me a couple of big dogs, who would talk to me with their eyes, so full of dumb thought, and together we would wander over the uplands, seeking our dinner, after the old primitive fashion of the men who dreamt not of ten-course dinners and Savoy suppers. I would cook the food myself, and sit down to the meal with a bottle of good wine, such as starts a man's thoughts (for I am inconsistent, as I acknowledge, and that gift of civilisation I would bear with me into my hermitage). Then in the evening, with pipe in mouth, beside my log-wood fire, I would sit and think, until new knowledge came to me. Strengthened by those silent voices that are drowned in the roar of Streetland, I might, perhaps, grow into something nearer to what it was intended that a man should be – might catch a glimpse, perhaps, of the meaning of life.

No, no, my dear lady, into this life of renunciation I would not take a companion, certainly not of the sex you are thinking of, even would she care to come, which I doubt. There are times when a man is better without the woman, when a woman is better without the man. Love drags us from the depths, makes men and women of us, but if we would climb a little nearer to the stars we must say goodbye to it. We men and women do not show ourselves to each other at our best; too often, I fear, at our worst. The woman's highest ideal of man is the lover; to a man the woman is always the possible beloved. We see each other's hearts, but not each other's souls. In each other's presence we never shake ourselves free from the earth. Matchmaking Mother Nature is always at hand to prompt us. A woman lifts us up into manhood, but there she would have us stay. 'Climb up to me,' she cries to the lad, walking with soiled feet in muddy ways, 'be a true man that you may be worthy to walk by my side. Be brave to protect me, kind and tender, and true, but climb no higher, stay here by my side.' The martyr, the prophet, the leader of the world's forlorn hopes, she would wake from his dream. Her arms she would fling about his neck holding him down.

To the woman the man says, 'You are my wife. Here is your America, within these walls, here is your work, your duty.' True, in nine hundred and ninety-nine cases out of every thousand, but men and women are not made in moulds, and the world's work is various. Sometimes to her sorrow, a woman's work lies beyond the home. The duty of Mary was not to Joseph.

The hero in the popular novel is the young man who says, 'I love you better than my soul.' Our favourite heroine in fiction is the woman who cries to her lover, 'I would go down into Hell to be with you.' There are men and women who cannot answer thus – the men who dream dreams, the women who see visions – impracticable people from the Bayswater point of view. But Bayswater would not be the abode of peace it is had it not been for such.

Have we not placed sexual love on a pedestal higher than it deserves? It is a noble passion, but it is not the noblest. There is a wider love by the side of which it is but as the lamp illumining the cottage, to the moonlight bathing the hills and valleys. There were two women once. This is a play I saw acted in the daylight. They had been friends from girlhood, till there came between them the usual trouble – a man. A weak, pretty creature not worth a thought from either of them – but women love the unworthy – there would be no over-population problem did they not, and this poor specimen, ill luck had ordained they should contend for.

Their rivalry brought out all that was worst in both of them. It is a mistake to suppose love only elevates: it can debase. It was a mean struggle for what to an onlooker must have appeared a remarkably unsatisfying prize. The loser might well have left the conqueror to her poor triumph, even granting it had been gained unfairly. But the old, ugly, primeval passions had been stirred in these women, and the wedding bells closed only the first act.

The second is not difficult to guess. It would have ended in the Divorce Court had not the deserted wife felt that a finer revenge would be secured to her by silence.

In the third, after an interval of only eighteen months, the man died – the first piece of good fortune that seems to have occurred to him personally throughout the play. His position must have been an exceedingly anxious one from the beginning. Notwithstanding his flabbiness, one cannot but regard him with a certain amount of pity not unmixed with amusement. Most of life's dramas can be viewed as either farce or tragedy according to the whim of the spectator. The actors invariably play them as tragedy, but then that is the essence of good farce acting.

Thus was secured the triumph of legal virtue and the punishment of irregularity, and the play might be dismissed as uninterestingly orthodox were it not for the fourth act, showing how the wronged wife came to the woman she had once wronged to ask and grant forgiveness. Strangely as it may sound, they found their love for one another unchanged. They had been long parted: it was sweet to hold each other's hands again. Two lonely women, they agreed to live together. Those who knew them well in this later time say that their life was very beautiful, filled with graciousness and nobility.

I do not say that such a story could ever be common, but it is more probable than the world might credit. Sometimes the man is better without the woman, the woman without the man.

On the Inadvisability of Following Advice

I was pacing the Euston platform late one winter's night, waiting for the last train to Watford, when I noticed a man cursing an automatic machine. Twice he shook his fist at it. I expected every moment to see him strike it. Naturally curious, I drew near softly. I wanted to catch what he was saying. However, he heard my approaching footsteps, and turned on me. 'Are you the man,' said he, 'who was here just now?'

'Just where?' I replied. I had been pacing up and down the platform for about five minutes.

'Why here, where we are standing,' he snapped out. 'Where do you think "here" is, over there?' He seemed irritable.

'I may have passed this spot in the course of my peregrinations, if that is what you mean,' I replied. I spoke with studied politeness; my idea was to rebuke his rudeness.

'I mean,' he answered, 'are you the man that spoke to me, just a minute ago?'

'I am not that man,' I said, 'goodnight.'

'Are you sure?' he persisted.

'One is not likely to forget talking to you,' I retorted.

His tone had been most offensive. 'I beg your pardon,' he replied grudgingly. 'I thought you looked like the man who spoke to me a minute or so ago.'

I felt mollified; he was the only other man on the platform, and I had a quarter of an hour to wait. 'No, it certainly wasn't me,' I returned genially, but ungrammatically. 'Why, did you want him?'

'Yes, I did,' he answered. 'I put a penny in the slot here,' he continued, feeling apparently the need of unburdening himself, 'wanted a box of matches. I couldn't get anything out, and I was shaking the machine, and swearing at it, as one does, when there came along a man, about your size, and – you're sure it wasn't you?'

'Positive,' I again ungrammatically replied, 'I would tell you if it had been. What did he do?'

'Well, he saw what had happened, or guessed it. He said, "They are troublesome things, those machines. They want understanding." I said, "They want taking up and flinging into the sea, that's what they want!" I was feeling mad because I hadn't a match about me, and I use a lot. He said, "They stick sometimes. The thing to do is to put another penny in; the weight of the first penny is not always sufficient. The second penny loosens the drawer and tumbles out itself; so that you get your purchase together with your first penny back again. I have often succeeded that way." Well, it seemed a silly explanation, but he talked as if he had been weaned by an automatic machine, and I was sawney enough to listen to him. I dropped in what I thought was another penny. I have just discovered it was a two-shilling piece. The fool was right to a certain extent, I have got something out. I have got this.' He held it towards me. I looked at it. It was a packet of Everton toffee.

'Two and a penny,' he remarked, bitterly. 'I'll sell it for a third of what it cost me.'

'You have put your money into the wrong machine,' I suggested.

'Well, I know that!' he answered, a little crossly, as it seemed to me – he was not a nice man: had there been any one else to talk to I should have left him. 'It isn't losing the money I mind so much, it's getting this damn thing that annoys me. If I could find that idiot I'd ram it down his throat.' We walked to the end of the platform, side by side, in silence.

'There are people like that,' he broke out, as we turned, 'people who will go about, giving advice. I'll be getting six months over one of them, I'm always afraid. I remember a pony I had once.' (I judged the man to be a small farmer; he talked in a wurzelly tone. I don't know if you understand what I mean, but an atmosphere of wurzels was the thing that somehow he suggested.) 'It was a thoroughbred Welsh pony, as sound a little beast as ever stepped. I'd had him out to grass all the winter, and one day in the early spring I thought I'd take him for a run. I had to go to Amersham on business. I put him into the cart, and drove him across – it is just ten miles from my place. He was a bit uppish, and had lathered himself pretty freely by the time we reached the town.

'A man was at the door of the hotel. He says, "That's a good pony of yours."

'"Pretty middling," I says. "It doesn't do to over-drive 'em, when they're young," he says.

'I says, "He's done ten miles, and I've done most of the pulling. I reckon I'm a jolly sight more exhausted than he is." I went inside and did my business, and when I came out the man was still there.

'"Going back up the hill?" he says to me. Somehow, I didn't cotton to him from the beginning.

'"Well, I've got to get the other side of it," I says, "and unless you know any patent way of getting over a hill without going up it, I reckon am."

'He says, "You take my advice: give him a pint of old ale before you start."

'"Old ale," I says, "why he's a teetotaler."

'"Never you mind that," he answers, "you give him a pint of old ale. I know these ponies: he's a good 'un, but he ain't set. A pint of old ale, and he'll take you up that hill like a cable tramway, and not hurt himself."

'I don't know what it is about this class of man. One asks oneself afterwards why one didn't knock his hat over his eyes and run his head into the nearest horse-trough. But at the time one listens to them. I got a pint of old ale in a hand-bowl, and brought it out. About half a dozen chaps were standing round, and of course there was a good deal of chaff.

'"You're starting him on the downward course, Jim," says one of them. "He'll take to gambling, rob a bank, and murder his mother. That's always the result of a glass of ale, 'cording to the tracts."

'"He won't drink it like that," says another, "it's as flat as ditchwater. Put a head on it for him."

'"Ain't you got a cigar for him?" says a third.

'"A cup of coffee and a round of buttered toast would do him a sight more good, a cold day like this," says a fourth.

'I'd half a mind then to throw the stuff away, or drink it myself. It seemed a piece of bally nonsense, giving good ale to a four-year-old pony, but the moment the beggar smelt the bowl he reached out his head, and lapped it up as though he'd been a Christian, and I jumped into the cart and started off, amid cheers. We got up the hill pretty steady. Then the liquor began to work into his head. I've taken home a drunken man more than once, and there's pleasanter jobs than that. I've seen a drunken woman, and they're worse. But a drunken Welsh pony I never want to have anything more to do with so long as I live. Having four legs he managed to hold himself up, but as to guiding himself, he couldn't, and as for letting me do it, he wouldn't. First we were one side of the road, and then we were the other. When we were not either side, we were crossways in the middle. I heard a bicycle bell behind me, but I dared not turn my head. All I could do was to shout to the fellow to keep where he was.

'"I want to pass you," he sang out, so soon as he was near enough.

'"Well, you can't do it," I called back.

'"Why can't I?" he answered. "How much of the road do you want?"

'"All of it and a bit over," I answered him, "for this job, and nothing in the way."

'He followed me for half a mile, abusing me, and every time he thought he saw a chance he tried to pass me. But the pony was always a bit too smart for him. You might have thought the brute was doing it on purpose.

'"You're not fit to be driving," he shouted. He was quite right, I wasn't. I was feeling just about dead beat.

'"What do you think you are?" he continued, "the charge of the Light Brigade?" (He was a common sort of fellow.) "Who sent you home with the washing?"

'Well, he was making me wild by this time. "What's the good of talking to me?" I shouted back. "Come and blackguard the pony if you want to blackguard anybody. I've got all I can do without the help of that alarm clock of yours. Go away, you're only making him worse."

'"What's the matter with the pony?" he called out.

'"Can't you see?" I answered. "He's drunk." Well, of course it sounded foolish. The truth often does.

'"One of you's drunk," he retorted, "for two pins I'd come and haul you out of the cart."

'I wish to goodness he had; I'd have given something to be out of that cart. But he didn't have the chance. At that moment the pony gave a sudden swerve, and I take it he must have been a bit too close. I heard a yell and a curse, and at the same instant I was splashed from head to foot with ditchwater. Then the brute bolted. A man was coming along, asleep on the top of a cartload of Windsor chairs. It's disgraceful the way those wagoners go to sleep – I wonder there are not more accidents. I don't think he ever knew what had happened to him. I couldn't look round to see what became of him, I only saw him start. Halfway down the hill a policeman holla'd to me to stop. I heard him shouting out something about furious driving. Half a mile this side of Chesham we came upon a girls' school walking two and two – a "crocodile" they call it, I think. I bet you those girls are still talking about it. It must have taken the old woman a good hour to collect them together again.

'It was market day in Chesham, and I guess there has not been a busier market day in Chesham before or since. We went through the town at about thirty miles an hour. I've never seen Chesham so lively, it's a sleepy hole as a rule. A mile outside the town I sighted the High Wycombe coach. I didn't feel I minded much. I had got to that pass when it didn't seem to matter to me what happened, I only felt curious. A dozen yards off the coach the pony stopped dead; that jerked me off the seat to the bottom of the cart. I couldn't get up, because the seat was on top of me. I could see nothing but the sky, and occasionally the head of the pony, when he stood upon his hind legs. But I could hear what the driver of the coach said, and I judged he was having trouble also.

'"Take that damn circus out of the road," he shouted. If he'd had any sense he'd have seen how helpless I was. I could hear his cattle plunging about. They are like that, horses, if they see one fool, then they all want to be fools.

'"Take it home, and tie it up to its organ," shouted the guard.

'Then an old woman went into hysterics, and began laughing like a hyena. That started the pony off again, and, as far as I could calculate by watching the clouds, we did about another four miles at the gallop. Then he thought he'd try to jump a gate, and finding, I suppose, that the cart hampered him, he started kicking it to pieces. I'd never have thought a cart could have been separated into so many pieces, if I hadn't seen it done. When he had got rid of everything but half a wheel and the splashboard he bolted again. I remained behind with the other ruins, and glad I was to get a little rest. He came back later in the afternoon, and I was pleased to sell him the next week for a five-pound note: it cost me about another ten to repair myself.

'To this day I am chaffed about that pony, and the local temperance society made a lecture out of me. That's what comes of following advice.'

I sympathised with him. I have suffered from advice myself. I have a friend, a city man, whom I meet occasionally. One of his most ardent passions in life is to make my fortune. He button-holes me in Threadneedle Street. 'The very man I wanted to see,' he says, 'I'm going to let you in for a good thing. We are getting up a little syndicate.' He is for ever 'getting up' a little syndicate, and for every hundred pounds you put into it you take a thousand out. Had I gone into all his little syndicates, I could have been worth at the present moment, I reckon, two million five hundred thousand pounds. But I have not gone into all his little syndicates. I went into one, years ago, when I was younger. I am still in it; my friend is confident that my holding, later on, will yield me thousands. Being, however, hard-up for ready money, I am willing to part with my share to any deserving person at a genuine reduction, upon a cash basis. Another friend of mine knows another man who is 'in the know' as regards racing matters. I suppose most people possess a friend of this type. He is generally very popular just before a race, and extremely unpopular immediately afterwards. A third benefactor of mine is an enthusiast upon the subject of diet. One day he brought me something in a packet, and pressed it into my hand with the air of a man who is relieving you of all your troubles.

'What is it?' I asked.

'Open it and see,' he answered, in the tone of a pantomime fairy. I opened it and looked, but I was no wiser.

'It's tea,' he explained.

'Oh!' I replied, 'I was wondering if it could be snuff.'

'Well, it's not exactly tea,' he continued, 'it's a sort of tea. You take one cup of that – one cup, and you will never care for any other kind of tea again.' He was quite right, I took one cup. After drinking it I felt I didn't care for any other tea. I felt I didn't care for anything, except to die quietly and inoffensively. He called on me a week later.

'You remember that tea I gave you?' he said.

'Distinctly,' I answered, 'I've got the taste of it in my mouth now.'

'Did it upset you?' he asked.

'It annoyed me at the time,' I answered, 'but that's all over now.'

He seemed thoughtful. 'You were quite correct,' he answered, 'it was snuff, a very special snuff, sent me all the way from India.'

'I can't say I liked it,' I replied.

'A stupid mistake of mine,' he went on, 'I must have mixed up the packets!'

'Oh, accidents will happen,' I said, 'and you won't make another mistake, I feel sure, so far as I am concerned.'

We can all give advice. I had the honour once of serving an old gentleman whose profession it was to give legal advice, and excellent legal advice he always gave. In common with most men who know the law, he had little respect for it. I have heard him say to a would-be litigant:

'My dear sir, if a villain stopped me in the street and demanded of me my watch and chain, I should refuse to give it to him. If he thereupon said, "Then I shall take it from you by brute force," I should, old as I am, I feel convinced, reply to him, "Come on." But if, on the other hand, he were to say to me, "Very well, then I shall take proceedings against you in the Court of Queen's Bench to compel you to give it up to me," I should at once take it from my pocket, press it into his hand, and beg of him to say no more about the matter. And I should consider I was getting off cheaply.'

Yet that same old gentleman went to law himself with his next-door neighbour over a dead poll parrot that wasn't worth sixpence to anybody, and spent from first to last a hundred pounds, if he spent a penny.

'I know I'm a fool,' he confessed. 'I have no positive proof that it was his cat, but I'll make him pay for calling me an Old Bailey Attorney, hanged if I don't!'

We all know how the pudding ought to be made. We do not profess to be able to make it: that is not our business. Our business is to criticise the cook. It seems our business to criticise so many things that it is not our business to do. We are all critics nowadays. I have my opinion of you, Reader, and you possibly have your own opinion of me. I do not seek to know it; personally, I prefer the man who says what he has to say of me behind my back. I remember, when on a lecturing tour, the groundplan of the hall often necessitated my mingling with the audience as they streamed out. This never happened but I would overhear somebody in front of me whisper to his or her companion, 'Take care, he's just behind you.' I always felt so grateful to that whisperer.

At a bohemian club, I was once drinking coffee with a novelist, who happened to be a broad-shouldered, athletic man. A fellow member, joining us, said to the novelist, 'I have just finished that last book of yours. I'll tell you my candid opinion of it.' Promptly replied the novelist, 'I give you fair warning, if you do, I shall punch your head.' We never heard that candid opinion.

Most of our leisure time we spend sneering at one another. It is a wonder, going about as we do with our noses so high in the air, we do not walk off this little round world into space, all of us. The masses sneer at the classes. The morals of the classes are shocking. If only the classes would consent as a body to be taught behaviour by committee of the masses, how very much better it would be for them. If only the classes would neglect their own interests and devote themselves to the welfare of the masses, the masses would be more pleased with them.

The classes sneer at the masses. If only the masses would follow the advice given them by the classes; if only they would be thrifty on their ten shillings a week; if only they would all be teetotalers, or drink old claret, which is not intoxicating; if only all the girls would be domestic servants on five pounds a year, and not waste their money on feathers; if only the men would be content to work for fourteen hours a day, and to sing in tune, 'God bless the Squire and his relations,' and would consent to be kept in their proper stations, all things would go swimmingly, for the classes.

The new woman pooh-poohs the old, the old woman is indignant with the new. The chapel denounces the stage, the stage ridicules little Bethel. The minor poet sneers at the world; the world laughs at the minor poet.

Man criticises Woman. We are not altogether pleased with woman. We discuss her shortcomings, we advise her for her good. If only English wives would dress as French wives, talk as American wives, cook as German wives! If only women would be precisely what we want them to be – patient and hardworking, brilliantly witty and exhaustively domestic, bewitching, amenable, and less suspicious – how very much better it would be for them, also for us. We work so hard to teach them, but they will not listen. Instead of paying attention to our wise counsel, the tiresome creatures are wasting their time criticising us. It is a popular game, this game of school. All that is needful is a doorstep, a cane, and six other children. The difficulty is the six other children. Every child wants to be the schoolmaster; they will keep jumping up, saying it is their turn.

Woman wants to take the stick now, and put man on the doorstep. There are one or two things she has got to say to him. He is not at all the man she approves of. He must begin by getting rid of all his natural desires and propensities. That done, she will take him in hand and make of him – not a man – but something very much superior.

It would be the best of all possible worlds if everybody would only follow our advice. I wonder, would Jerusalem have been the cleanly city it is reported, if, instead of troubling himself concerning his own twopenny-halfpenny doorstep, each citizen had gone out into the road and given eloquent lectures to all the other inhabitants on the subject of sanitation?

We have taken to criticising the Creator Himself of late. The world is wrong, we are wrong. If only He had taken our advice, during those first six days!

Why do I seem to have been scooped out and filled up with lead? Why do I hate the smell of bacon, and feel that nobody cares for me? It is because champagne and lobsters have been made wrong.

Why do Edwin and Angelina quarrel? It is because Edwin has been given a fine, high-spirited nature that will not brook contradiction, while Angelina, poor girl, has been cursed with contradictory instincts.

Why is excellent Mr Jones brought down next door to beggary? Mr Jones had an income of a thousand a year, secured by the funds. But there came along a wicked company promoter (why are wicked company promoters permitted?) with a prospectus, telling good Mr Jones how to obtain a hundred per cent for his money by investing it in some scheme for the swindling of Mr Jones' fellow citizens.

The scheme does not succeed. The people swindled turn out, contrary to the promise of the prospectus, to be Mr Jones and his fellow investors. Why does heaven allow these wrongs?

Why does Mrs Brown leave her husband and children, to run off with the new doctor? It is because an ill-advised creator has given Mrs Brown and the new doctor unduly strong emotions. Neither Mrs Brown nor the new doctor are to be blamed. If any human being be answerable it is, probably, Mrs Brown's grandfather, or some early ancestor of the new doctor's.

We shall criticise heaven when we get there. I doubt if any of us will be pleased with the arrangements, we have grown so exceedingly critical.

It was once said of a very superior young man that he seemed to be under the impression that God Almighty had made the universe chiefly to hear what he would say about it. Consciously or unconsciously, most of us are of this way of thinking. It is an age of mutual improvement societies – a delightful idea, everybody's business being to improve everybody else – of amateur parliaments, of literary councils, of playgoers' clubs.

First night criticism seems to have died out of late, the student of the drama having come to the conclusion, possibly, that plays are not worth criticising. But in my young days we were very earnest at this work. We went to the play, less with the selfish desire of enjoying our evening, than with the noble aim of elevating the stage. Maybe we did good, maybe we were needed – let us think so. Certain it is, many of the old absurdities have disappeared from the theatre, and our rough-and-ready criticism may have helped the happy dispatch. A folly is often served by an unwise remedy.

The dramatist in those days had to reckon with his audience. Gallery and pit took an interest in his work such as galleries and pits no longer take. I recollect witnessing the production of a very blood-curdling melodrama at, I think, the old Queen's Theatre. The heroine had been given by the author a quite unnecessary amount of conversation, so we considered. The woman, whenever she appeared on the stage, talked by the yard. She could not do a simple little thing like cursing the villain under about twenty lines. When the hero asked her if she loved him she stood up and made a speech about it that lasted three minutes by the watch. One dreaded to see her open her mouth. In the third act, somebody got hold of her and shut her up in a dungeon. He was not a nice man, speaking generally, but we felt he was the man for the situation, and the house cheered him to the echo. We flattered ourselves we had got rid of her for the rest of the evening. Then some fool of a turnkey came along, and she appealed to him, through the grating, to let her out for a few minutes. The turnkey, a good but soft-hearted man, hesitated.

'Don't you do it,' shouted one earnest student of the drama, from the gallery, 'she's all right. Keep her there!'

The old idiot paid no attention to our advice; he argued the matter to himself. ''Tis but a trifling request,' he remarked, 'and it will make her happy.'

'Yes, but what about us?' replied the same voice from the gallery. 'You don't know her. You've only just come on, we've been listening to her all the evening. She's quiet now, you let her be.'

'Oh, let me out, if only for one moment!' shrieked the poor woman. 'I have something that I must say to my child.'

'Write it on a bit of paper, and pass it out,' suggested a voice from the pit. 'We'll see that he gets it.'

'Shall I keep a mother from her dying child?' mused the turnkey. 'No, it would be inhuman.'

'No, it wouldn't,' persisted the voice of the pit, 'not in this instance. It's too much talk that has made the poor child ill.'

The turnkey would not be guided by us. He opened the cell door amidst the execrations of the whole house. She talked to her child for about five minutes, at the end of which time it died.

'Ah, he is dead!' shrieked the distressed parent.

'Lucky beggar!' was the unsympathetic rejoinder of the house.

Sometimes the criticism of the audience would take the form of remarks, addressed by one gentleman to another. We had been listening one night to a play in which action seemed to be unnecessarily subordinated to dialogue, and somewhat poor dialogue at that. Suddenly, across the wearying talk from the stage, came the stentorian whisper:

'Jim!'

'Hallo!'

'Wake me up when the play begins.' This was followed by an ostentatious sound as of snoring. Then the voice of the second speaker was heard:

'Sammy!' His friend appeared to awake.

'Eh? Yes? What's up? Has anything happened?'

'Wake you up at half-past eleven in any event, I suppose?'

'Thanks, do, sonny.' And the critic slept again.

Yes, we took an interest in our plays then. I wonder shall I ever enjoy the British drama again as I enjoyed it in those days? Shall I ever enjoy a supper again as I enjoyed the tripe and onions washed down with bitter beer at the bar of the old Albion? I have tried many suppers after the theatre since then, and some, when friends have been in generous mood, have been expensive and elaborate. The cook may have come from Paris, his portrait may be in the illustrated papers, his salary may be reckoned by hundreds, but there is something wrong with his art, for all that, I miss a flavour in his meats. There is a sauce lacking.

Nature has her coinage, and demands payment in her own currency. At Nature's shop it is you yourself must pay. Your unearned increment, your inherited fortune, your luck, are not legal tenders across her counter.

You want a good appetite. Nature is quite willing to supply you. 'Certainly, sir,' she replies, 'I can do you a very excellent article indeed. I have here a real genuine hunger and thirst that will make your meal a delight to you. You shall eat heartily and with zest, and you shall rise from the table refreshed, invigorated, and cheerful.'

'Just the very thing I want,' exclaims the gourmet delightedly. 'Tell me the price.'

'The price,' answers Mrs Nature, 'is one long day's hard work.'

The customer's face falls. He handles nervously his heavy purse.

'Cannot I pay for it in money?' he asks. 'I don't like work, but I am a rich man, I can afford to keep French cooks, to purchase old wines.'

Nature shakes her head.

'I cannot take your cheques, tissue and nerve are my charges. For these I can give you an appetite that will make a rump-steak and a tankard of ale more delicious to you than any dinner that the greatest chef in Europe could put before you. I can even promise you that a hunk of bread and cheese shall be a banquet to you, but you must pay my price in my money, I do not deal in yours.'

And next the dilettante enters, demanding a taste for art and literature, and this also Nature is quite prepared to supply.

'I can give you true delight in all these things,' she answers. 'Music shall be as wings to you, lifting you above the turmoil of the world. Through art you shall catch a glimpse of truth. Along the pleasant paths of literature you shall walk as beside still waters.'

'And your charge?' cries the delighted customer.

'These things are somewhat expensive,' replies Nature. 'I want from you a life lived simply, free from all desire of worldly success, a life from which passion has been lived out, a life to which appetite has been subdued.'

'But you mistake, my dear lady,' replies the dilettante, 'I have many friends, possessed of taste, and they are men who do not pay this price for it. Their houses are full of beautiful pictures, they rave about "nocturnes" and "symphonies", their shelves are packed with first editions. Yet they are men of luxury and wealth and fashion. They trouble much concerning the making of money, and society is their heaven. Cannot I be as one of these?'

'I do not deal in the tricks of apes,' answers Nature coldly, 'the culture of these friends of yours is a mere pose, a fashion of the hour, their talk mere parrot chatter. Yes, you can purchase such culture as this, and pretty cheaply, but a passion for skittles would be of more service to you, and bring you more genuine enjoyment. My goods are of a different class. I fear we waste each other's time.'

And next comes the boy, asking with a blush for love, and Nature's motherly old heart goes out to him, for it is an article she loves to sell, and she loves those who come to purchase it of her. So she leans across the counter, smiling, and tells him that she has the very thing he wants, and he, trembling with excitement, likewise asks the figure.

'It costs a good deal,' explains Nature, but in no discouraging tone, 'it is the most expensive thing in all my shop.'

'I am rich,' replies the lad. 'My father worked hard and saved, and he has left me all his wealth. I have stocks and shares, and lands and factories, and will pay any price in reason for this thing.'

But Nature, looking graver, lays her hand upon his arm. 'Put by your purse, boy,' she says, 'my price is not a price in reason, nor is gold the metal that I deal in. There are many shops in various streets where your banknotes will be accepted. But if you will take an old woman's advice, you will not go to them. The thing they will sell you will bring sorrow and do evil to you. It is cheap enough, but, like all things cheap, it is not worth the buying. No man purchases it, only the fool.'

'And what is the cost of the thing you sell then?' asks the lad.

'Self-forgetfulness, tenderness, strength,' answers the old Dame, 'the love of all things that are of good repute, the hate of all things evil, courage, sympathy, self-respect, these things purchase love. Put by your purse, lad, it will serve you in other ways, but it will not buy for you the goods upon my shelves.'

'Then am I no better off than the poor man?' demands the lad.

'I know not wealth or poverty as you understand it,' answers Nature. 'Here I exchange realities only for realities. You ask for my treasures, I ask for your brain and heart in exchange – yours, boy, not your father's, not another's.'

'And this price,' he argues, 'how shall I obtain it?'

'Go about the world,' replies the great lady. 'Labour, suffer, help. Come back to me when you have earned your wages, and according to how much you bring me so we will do business.'

Is real wealth so unevenly distributed as we think? Is not fate the true socialist? Who is the rich man, who the poor? Do we know? Does even the man himself know? Are we not striving for the shadow, missing the substance? Take life at its highest: which was the happier man, rich Solomon or poor Socrates? Solomon seems to have had most things that most men most desire, maybe too much of some for his own comfort. Socrates had little beyond what he carried about with him, but that was a good deal. According to our scales, Solomon should have been one of the happiest men that ever lived, Socrates one of the most wretched. But was it so?

Or taking life at its lowest, with pleasure its only goal. Is my lord Tom Noddy, in the stalls, so very much jollier than 'Arry in the gallery? Were beer ten shillings the bottle, and champagne fourpence a quart, which, think you, we should clamour for? If every West End club had its skittle alley, and billiards could only be played in East End pubs, which game, my lord, would you select? Is the air of Berkeley Square so much more joy-giving than the atmosphere of Seven Dials? I find myself a piquancy in the air of Seven Dials, missing from Berkeley Square. Is there so vast a difference between horsehair and straw, when you are tired? Is happiness multiplied by the number of rooms in one's house? Are Lady Ermintrude's lips so very much sweeter than Sally's of the Alley? What is success in life?

Notes

1. A legal term derived from Latin, meaning 'in the character or manner of a pauper'.
2. The *unco guid* are those who are self-avowedly strict in matters of religious or moral significance.

Biographical note

The son of an unsuccessful ironmonger, Jerome Klapka Jerome was born in Walsall, Staffordshire, in 1859, where his family remained until 1861. Following the collapse of their business, they relocated to Stourbridge and then to Poplar in East London, where Jerome was brought up in relative poverty.

Jerome left school at fourteen and worked variously as a clerk, a journalist, an actor and a schoolmaster. In 1885 he published his first book, *On the Stage and Off*, a collection of humorous pieces about the theatre. This was followed in 1886 by *The Idle Thoughts of an Idle Fellow*, another set of comic essays. Two years later, Jerome married Elizabeth Henrietta Stanley Marris. They spent their honeymoon on the Thames and on their return, Jerome began the work with which he achieved lasting fame, *Three Men in a Boat* (1889). In 1892 Jerome and some friends founded *The Idler*, a humorous magazine that published works by Mark Twain and W.W. Jacobs among others. Further works included *Three Men on the Bummel*, which described a tour in Germany, *Paul Klever* (1902), an autobiographical novel, and the play *Passing of the Third Floor Back* (1908).

Jerome's autobiography, *My Life and Times*, was published in 1926 and shortly afterwards he was made a Freeman of the Borough of Walsall. He died after suffering a stroke in 1927 and is buried in Ewelme in Oxfordshire.